Country weekend entertaining

by the same author

LOAVES AND FISHES

THE LOAVES AND FISHES PARTY COOKBOOK

Anna Pump

with Gen LeRoy

PHOTOGRAPHS BY CHRIS MEADE

Country

Doubleday   NEW YORK   LONDON   TORONTO   SYDNEY   AUCKLAND

Seasonal recipes

FROM LOAVES AND FISHES
AND THE BRIDGEHAMPTON INN

weekend

DISCARD

entertaining

PUBLISHED BY DOUBLEDAY
a division of Random House, Inc.
1540 Broadway, New York, New York 10036

DOUBLEDAY and the portrayal of an anchor with a dolphin are
trademarks of Doubleday, a division of Random House, Inc.

BOOK DESIGN BY MARIA CARELLA
ILLUSTRATIONS BY ANDREA BROOKS

Library of Congress Cataloging-in-Publication Data
Pump, Anna.
Country weekend entertaining: seasonal recipes from Loaves and Fishes and the
Bridgehampton Inn / Anna Pump with Gen LeRoy. — 1st ed.
p.   cm.
Includes index.
1. Entertaining.   2. Cookery.   3. Loaves and Fishes (Store: Sagaponack, N.Y.)
4. Bridgehampton Inn.   I. LeRoy, Gen.   II. Loaves and Fishes (Store: Sagaponack, N.Y.)
III. Bridgehampton Inn.   IV. Title.   TX731.P84   1999
642′.4—dc21   98-8311
CIP

ISBN 0-385-48827-0

Acknowledgments

Gen and I have always shared a love of good living and fine eating. Thank you so much, Gen; without that common bond, there could have been no book. There are others I wish to thank: Arlene Friedman and Alison Bond, who originally approached us about this book, and then gave it wings; Chris Meade, who enriched these pages with his creative and original photographic eye. Judy Kern was terrific—her trust and her enthusiasm for the project, coupled with her sound advice, never flagged.

Thanks to Sybille Pump for her total support and for keeping our busy store and catering business at Loaves and Fishes on track—also for her Grilled Chicken Salad recipe. And where would I be without Maureen Brown and Cerene DeSilva, who kept the Bridgehampton Inn running smoothly while I tested and retested all the recipes? Thanks to Bridget LeRoy and Emma Walton for editing the final drafts, and very special thanks to my husband, Detlef Pump, and Gen's husband, Tony Walton, whose unconditional support allowed Gen and I to tackle this book with unbridled devotion and determination. It's been great fun all the way!

ANNA PUMP

Contents

Spring and Summer

Fall and Winter

Country weekend entertaining

Introduction

....

I believe that my passion for cooking and my joy of entertaining were instilled at a very early age. My mother never entertained fewer than fifteen people at one time. Friends, neighbors, relatives, field hands, all seated around a large bountiful table she set up either in our living room or, in more clement weather, outside under a large spreading tree.

I grew up on a large working farm in Tarp, Germany, close to the Danish border, where we cultivated crops of potatoes, wheat, and vegetables; had a variety of fruit trees; and raised cows, pigs, chickens, and geese. It was during those formative years that I learned how to make sausages, smoke meats, salt fresh fish, churn butter, and make cheeses. In the fall, we converted baskets of fruit into preserves, jams, and sauces that helped to remind us of summer during our long, relentlessly frigid Scandinavian winters. The sealed jars of fruits, pickles, and vegetables lined the shelves in our basement next to bins of rutabagas, carrots, onions, and potatoes.

It was no less busy in winter after the farm closed down. My parents went regularly to the opera in Flensburg, arriving home with neighbors and friends. Food would appear as if by magic: decanters of wine, superb desserts. It was a bustling time when entertaining was elevated to new heights. My mother was an excellent cook, both daring and inventive. Dinners were large, boisterous, and happy, with flickering candles set about the room. The fireplaces, alive and crackling, created just the right combination of warmth and excitement. Those early days certainly defined my life as it is today.

After schooling, I married and, soon after, my husband Detlef and I started our own family. With our two children in tow, we moved to America where I worked as a caterer, creating recipes with an array of new herbs, vegetables, and foods that absolutely dazzled me. We made frequent trips to France, Italy, Germany, Mexico, and, when traveling by car, discovered marvelous bed and break-

fasts and hotels, both quaint and luxurious. With every journey I was able to sample traditional dishes, new and exotic foods, choosing those that, with a little adjustment, would eventually round out my growing catalogue of recipes.

After a few years I began to yearn for a new challenge, and that was when, with my daughter, Sybille, a marvelous cook, I opened Loaves and Fishes in Sagaponack, Long Island. We have both had a great time and have met many wonderful people—customers who are now our friends. Although we have an extensive take-out department, we also cater dinners, lunches, brunches, cocktail parties, weddings, funerals, graduations, social gatherings that range anywhere from twelve to five hundred people, sometimes on the same day. I suppose that is why so many people stared at me, utterly amazed, when I announced that I had been seriously thinking of opening a bed and breakfast.

It was the building itself that had always intrigued me. Sitting off Main Street in Bridgehampton, it rose above the towering boxwoods that nearly obscured it from view. I would pass it daily, either on my way to Loaves and Fishes, which is about a mile away, or on my way home from catering a party, and always found myself slowing down to see if I could get a better look.

One day, my curiosity won out and I stopped. I had already learned that it was built as a private residence by one of the first families to settle in Bridgehampton and that at one time it had been an inn. I had to squeeze past the boxwoods that had swelled across the entrance. The path was overwhelmed by vines and rambling bushes, but beyond the bushes stood an eighteenth-century house, stately yet homey, elegantly scaled, graceful, and—most important—welcoming. I immediately loved it.

I circled the building, peering into windows that were nearly opaque with grime. I made out a staircase leading to the second floor, and as I moved farther around, I could see into a large kitchen. Beyond that was a wonderfully spacious living room with a fireplace tucked into one corner, graced with French windows that opened onto a terrace. Perfect. The building itself was badly in need of paint but to me, the setting, the proportions, the beauty were exactly what I had hoped they'd be.

I stood in the back gazing out at the garden. Although the town was drenched with sun, it seemed several degrees cooler back there. Lofty elms, an assortment of spreading maple trees, some Norway spruces, all somehow generated a pleasant breeze. I could see exactly where the herb garden would go, where to plant the rose bushes, where we could set up two marquees for private parties, under which tree to place the picnic table, how many tables would fit comfortably on the bricked terrace for morning coffees or twilight drinks. My heart was hammering as I turned back toward Loaves and Fishes. This was what I had been wanting for a very long time; to create a wonderful environment in which I could treat guests to home-

cooked meals, prepared in the Inn's vast kitchen and served in rooms I intended to be as comfortable and inviting as possible. In other words, a home away from home where I could entertain guests the way I myself would like to be entertained.

As I headed back to Loaves and Fishes, I thought about the similarities between this marvelous village in which we had chosen to live and the farm where I was born. Flensburg is on a peninsula, with the Baltic on one side and the North Sea on the other and rolling farmlands connecting the two coastlines. Here, at the tip of Long Island, we have the Atlantic on one side, with its glistening white beaches, and the Long Island Sound on the other, and connecting the two coastlines are seven miles of splendidly arable land. It seemed right for me to want to re-create something tangible from all those marvelous memories.

I couldn't wait to get back and start the ball rolling. Sybille and I made a series of calls, and that afternoon we made an offer that, to our utter delight, was soon accepted. What followed next was a whirl of activity—planning, making list upon list. Unlocking the front door with my own key and stepping into the Inn for the first time filled me with excitement. I simply could not get the smile off my face as I moved from room to room, deciding just where and how to make the changes that would transform this gorgeous building into the Inn of my dreams.

Whoe'er had traveled Life's dull round,
Where'er his stages may have been,
May sigh to think he still has found
The warmest welcome, at an Inn.

WILLIAM SHENSTONE

Putting it together

·····································

*I*t was clear that the very first task would be to make the exterior of the Inn look as inviting as possible. This meant landscaping the front and sides, supplanting dead bushes with new ones, organizing flower beds, removing the massive wall of boxwoods and replacing it with a beautiful white picket fence. We graveled an area designated for cars and created a brick walkway from the sidewalk to our front door. Once that was done, Detlef set to work giving the clapboards a much-needed coat of paint. The result was magical. The Inn at last took its rightful place as one of the more distinguished buildings lining Bridgehampton's Main Street.

The inside was an altogether different matter. An initial stroll-through revealed a slight floor-buckling in the room I had imagined would be ideal for morning breakfasts. Detlef replaced the sagging beam in the basement and miraculously the original wooden floorboards relaxed and straightened out. We put in central air conditioning—a major plus during the more torrid summer days—and double-glazed all the windows.

After we had dealt with the basic structural work, we decided to start at the top and work our way down to the main floor. The original Inn had thirteen small bedrooms, ten on the upper floor, three in the attic, and six bathrooms. We decided that the rooms should be larger and immediately began to remove walls, build new ones, move doorways, restore the fireplaces, tear down wallpaper, but, most importantly, we were determined never to compromise the integrity of the structure. By the time the dust cleared, we had eight bedrooms, each with its own bathroom. We installed large European shower heads in each bathroom and adjusted the *plumbing to make sure there would be constant hot water. Detlef cut out marble*

tops for each new basin, insuring our guests room for their toilet bags, hair dryers,

and other necessities. We took down beautiful old sconces, discovered they were

solid brass, had them cleaned, and put them back on the walls.

For days, Sybille and I wandered through the rooms, soaking in the personal-
ity of each one, trying to decide how they should be decorated. Some had charm-
ing windows, inviting fireplaces, carvings over the doorways and doorframes.
Detlef felt that one should be decorated in an Americana style, with a Native
American rug, a four-poster bed, and quilts. A grander room was the perfect set-
ting for a gorgeous Beidemeier bedroom set. Those walls we painted a Hunter
Green to set off the blond furniture, and chose tone-on-tone beige curtains for the

windows. Another room we decided to paint sunny yellow, which would be set off

with crisp blue-and-white curtains and chair coverings.

As it started to come together before our eyes, it gave all of us a surge of en-

ergy. We found someone to build new four-poster beds—since antique beds can't

really take the wear and tear of an Inn—and while they were being constructed we

set about hunting for quilts, dressers, mirrors, tables, chairs, loveseats, and lamps.

We scoured our local area, crisscrossed Massachusetts, and wove our way through

the Pennsylvania countryside. We took a trip to Europe and found wonderful

chairs and tables in the town where I was born. We brought back carpets, rugs, side

tables, and Belgian cotton linens for all the beds. We chose fabrics at Laura Ashley

and ordered curtains to be made and sent. We raided our own store rooms and found ideal furniture that we had packed away when we moved into a smaller house. Phones and televisions were the final touch.

I would linger for a time after each room was completed, feeling what it would be like if I were a guest for the evening. It was important to make sure there was enough light for reading, yet equally important to retain the romantic atmosphere. I remember that while Sybille and I were inspecting each room, we'd catch each other's smiles, which, of course, made us smile even more.

Once the main stairway was carpeted, we went to work on the reception area, kitchen, dining room, and living room. The dimensions of the kitchen were quite adequate, but we needed new stoves and more ovens. We also had to buy a larger refrigerator to accommodate our guests' needs. After a good scrubbing and several coats of paint, the room looked terrific.

I remembered a delightful bed and breakfast in Arles, France, where Detlef and I once stayed. It was lovely to have an intimate table for just the two of us, where we could read, write postcards, or chat about our plans for the day. That was what I wanted for our breakfast room; tables that would accommodate two to four people, or could easily be assembled into various combinations for whatever number of guests needed to be seated together. I was so happy with our dining room. It was ideal for breakfasts because it caught the early morning sun as it splashed across the room. It also had a lovely fireplace that would be in constant use during the winter months. We built a small brick patio right outside the breakfast room that we felt would be perfect for breakfasts served out of doors. This meant our guests would have four choices: breakfast in bed, in our dining room, on the patio outside the dining room, or on the lovely shadier brick terrace that ran the length of the living room and was soon to be equipped with wicker furniture.

The living room needed painting. The floors needed sanding and staining. I *chose a dark wood grain color to set off the carpets we had bought in Europe, and*

planned several sitting areas for those guests who wanted to settle down in front of

the fire to read or work, and other areas where guests might want to entertain their

company. Large potted plants helped section off these areas. The room was spacious

and comfortable. As we discovered later, it could easily seat forty-eight for a sit-

down dinner. We chose artwork for the walls lit by more of the same wonderful

brass sconces we had cleaned and reinstalled. We set lamps in strategic spots, lit the

fire, and then took seats throughout the room. It was perfect. All it needed was

flower arrangements.

Sybille and I decided that, as the food would be fresh from our kitchen, so

should the flowers be fresh from our garden. In the winter we would plant indoor tubs and use those flowers in all the rooms and for all the individual breakfast tables. Freesia in late winter, tulips and daffodils in spring, roses in the summer, and cyclamen in late fall and early winter. We set up a fax machine in the reception area, polished the brass, found a loveseat covered in gorgeous Italian fabric, put a console table in the front entranceway, and all the time tried to remain mindful of what we might have missed. Yes, it looked ready. And yes, there had been glitches along the way, but all in all, everything had come together splendidly. And, oh yes, of course, it had been hard work that required a lot of inspiration and even more diligence, but we had loved every minute of it.

As I cautiously spoke the words, "I think we're ready," the phone rang. We looked from one to another. I reached for it before it rang a second time. Amazingly *it turned out to be our first guest calling for a reservation. They would be here at 5 P.M. This was exciting. The kitchen was stocked with food. Tables were set, silverware polished, crystal clean and sparkling, beds made. All that was needed was to get ourselves cleaned up and dressed. Detlef and I raced home. Sybille hurried back to Loaves and Fishes. We returned just before 5 to find an unfamiliar car already parked in the driveway. Then we saw our guests heading up the walk to meet us. Before I could apologize for not being there to greet them, they smiled and the husband said, "We got here two hours early." His wife added, "This place reminds me of home. Not my home, specifically, but the kind of home I dream of having."*

I couldn't imagine a more perfect reaction from our very first guests. I thanked them, opened the door, turned on the lights, and warmly welcomed them to our Inn.

Go, little book, and wish to all
Flowers in the garden, meat in the hall,
A bin of wine, a spice of wit,
A house with lawns enclosing it.

ROBERT LOUIS STEVENSON

Spring

and

Summer

. . . .

spring and summer
Breakfasts

....

*I*n many ways, breakfast seems to be the most important meal of the day because, with all the right components, it has the potential to start one's day on the right path. To awaken to the enticing aroma of fresh coffee wafting up from the kitchen, intermingled with the seductive smells of bacon or sausages sizzling on a griddle and the sweet scent of muffins baking in the oven—all combines to stir your senses and encourages you to feel that all may be right with the world.

In the spring and summer we are blessed with nature's bounty. Naturally ripened fruits send out the most intoxicating and inviting bouquets—succulent strawberries and raspberries, picked hours earlier, heaped into a bowl with a pitcher of cream on the side is, sometimes, as good as it gets. Fresh peaches, plums, cherries, and nectarines produce just the right perfumes and tastes to rouse the palate and, for me, evoke the most glorious of childhood memories. Therefore, one of our main priorities at the Inn is to make sure that fresh fruit is always accessible, abundant, and varied.

We have always felt that breakfast should be relaxed at the Inn. Some guests, arriving late the night before, request breakfast in bed. We send up a tray of freshly brewed coffee or a pot of tea, fresh-squeezed orange juice, a basket of sweet rolls hot from the oven, lots of creamy butter, and a dish of homemade preserves. Our guests also get a variety of papers, the local ones as well as the New York dailies, which Detlef collects each morning from a store nearby.

We always have classical music playing softly in the background. Tables are set up in the dining room or outside on the terrace with its wicker furniture, green-and-white-striped cushions, vivid blue creamers, and bright yellow sugar bowls that at first glance look like daffodils. Colorful linens and napkins, a small vase of

fresh flowers displayed as a centerpiece, all work in harmony to create a pleasant,
warm environment.

We glaze and bake a Virginia ham each Friday to last through the weekend.
The bone is made into soup on Monday. We have bacon; a full array of homemade
sausages; plenty of local farm-fresh eggs; waffle batter in the fridge, ready to go;
croissants baking in the oven, as well as fresh fruit muffins and scones. We change
the menu each week, which is not to say that there aren't also those occasions when
a guest can only manage a boiled egg, which of course, we gladly provide. We have
found that breakfast is a time when our guests like to linger—reading papers; chat-
ting; having a second, even a third cup of coffee; and often, since a certain amount
of time has elapsed, requesting a second waffle or another scone.

We have had families arrive the morning after a wedding party, which often-

times we had catered, to visit with relatives staying at the Inn. It has never presented a problem: We merely connect tables on the terrace or under the shade of a tree, whip up more batter, slice more ham, brew another pot of coffee, and are thrilled to hear contented laughter floating in from outside. And, once again, breakfast is transformed into the gentle dawning of a beautiful day.

> We may live without poetry, music and art;
> We may live without conscience, and live without heart;
> We may live without friends; we may live without books;
> But civilized man cannot live without cooks.

OWEN MEREDITH

Swedish pancakes
with warm blueberry sauce

A gorgeous sauce that's a breeze to make and will keep up to a week in the refrigerator. Drizzle it over a pound cake or pour it, warmed, over a mound of ice cream.

THE PANCAKES

3 eggs
2 cups milk
1 cup flour
$^1/_2$ teaspoon salt
5 tablespoons melted butter
6 tablespoons clarified butter (see box)

THE SAUCE

$1^1/_2$ tablespoons cornstarch
$^1/_2$ cup water
$^3/_4$ cup sugar
6 cups fresh blueberries
1 tablespoon lemon juice
$^1/_2$ teaspoon ground cinnamon

To make the pancakes, in a large bowl, whisk the eggs for 30 seconds. Add the milk, flour, and salt. Stir until smooth. Add the melted butter and stir until all the lumps are gone and the batter appears satiny.

Heat a 10-inch nonstick skillet over medium heat. Add 1 tablespoon of the clarified butter. Tilt the pan to coat the bottom completely. Fill a $^1/_4$-cup measure, three quarters full of pancake batter and pour into the hot pan. Repeat this procedure until you have 3 pancakes cooking at one time. When the edges begin to brown, turn the pancakes and continue cooking for 1 or 2 minutes longer, until the pancakes are nicely browned on both sides. They will be very thin, so fold them in half and layer them onto a warm dinner plate. Repeat with the rest of the batter until you have 18 pancakes.

To make the sauce, in a heavy saucepan, blend the cornstarch, water, and sugar. Add 3 cups of the blueberries. Bring to a simmer over medium heat. Stirring constantly, simmer until the sauce lightly thickens. Remove from the heat and add the remaining 3 cups of blueberries, the lemon juice and cinnamon. Stir to blend. Serve the sauce warm over the pancakes.

YIELDS 6 SERVINGS

CLARIFIED BUTTER

IN A SMALL SAUCEPAN OVER LOW HEAT, MELT 2 STICKS (1 CUP) OF BUTTER. SKIM THE FOAM FROM THE TOP. POUR THE CLEAR BUTTER INTO A CROCK, LEAVING AND DISCARDING THE MILKY RESIDUE. COVERED AND REFRIGERATED, IT WILL KEEP FOR UP TO 3 WEEKS.

Waffles

Waffles always remind me of my childhood. Summertime was when my parents took us for trips into the city, where we would find Belgian waffle stands on many of the busy street corners. My treat was to have a freshly made waffle filled with soft vanilla ice cream and topped with a scoop of fresh strawberries. We like to serve the waffles with seasonal fresh fruit and lightly whipped cream.

2^1/$_4$ cups flour
2 tablespoons sugar
Grated rind of 1 lemon
^{1}/$_4$ teaspoon salt
6 tablespoons melted butter, plus 1 tablespoon to brush
    the waffle iron
3 large eggs, separated
1^3/$_4$ cups milk

In a bowl, place the flour, sugar, lemon rind, and salt. Add the 6 tablespoons of butter, the egg yolks, and milk. Beat with a wire whisk until smooth. Beat the egg whites with an electric mixer until soft peaks hold. Fold the egg whites into the waffle batter.

Preheat the waffle iron for 10 minutes. Brush lightly with the tablespoon of butter. Ladle in enough batter to cover the grid. Close the lid and bake for 4 to 5 minutes. Continue with the remaining batter. Since the waffles will not stick once the iron is hot, there will be no need to butter it again.

YIELDS 8 TO 10 WAFFLES,
DEPENDING ON THE SIZE OF YOUR PAN

Scrambled eggs with cream cheese, fresh chives, and popovers

This is great with Oven-Crisp Bacon (see box) and homemade Strawberry Preserves (recipe follows).

THE POPOVERS

5 tablespoons butter
4 eggs
2 cups milk
1³/₄ cups flour
1 teaspoon salt

SCRAMBLED EGGS

2 tablespoons butter
8 eggs
¹/₂ teaspoon salt
3 ounces cream cheese, cut into small cubes
1 tablespoon finely chopped fresh chives

Preheat the oven to 450°F.

To make the popovers, in a small pan, melt the butter. Spoon 1 teaspoon of the butter into each of 12 nonstick muffin cups. Discard the remaining butter. Place in the oven for 3 minutes.

Using a wire whisk, beat the 4 eggs in a bowl. Add the milk, flour, and salt. Beat until smooth. Pour the batter into the 12 heated muffin tins, filling them two thirds full. Bake for 15 minutes. Lower the heat to 400° and bake for

15 minutes longer. Do not open the oven door during the baking time or the popovers may not rise properly.

To make the eggs, melt the butter in a large skillet over medium heat. Crack the eggs into a bowl, add the salt, and beat until smooth. Pour into the hot skillet. Scatter the cream cheese cubes over the eggs. Scramble gently until just set. Transfer the scrambled eggs to a large serving platter and sprinkle the top with chives.

SERVES 4 TO 6

OVEN-CRISP BACON

PREHEAT THE OVEN TO 300°F. SPREAD THICK BACON IN 1 LAYER ON A SHEET PAN. BAKE FOR 1 HOUR, UNTIL GOLDEN BROWN. DRAIN ON PAPER TOWELS. REHEAT IN THE OVEN OR IN A SKILLET AS NEEDED.

YORKSHIRE PUDDING

POUR THE POPOVER BATTER INTO A GREASED BAKING PAN AND PLACE IT IN A PREHEATED 450°F. OVEN FOR 30 MINUTES. DO NOT OPEN THE OVEN DOOR DURING BAKING TIME. THE PUDDING IS GREAT WITH ROAST BEEF.

Strawberry preserves

We use very ripe strawberries for this recipe, which will yield six to seven jars of preserves that can be sealed and stored in the refrigerator.

> **10 cups hulled strawberries**
> **5¹/₂ cups sugar**
> **2 tablespoons lemon juice**
> **¹/₂ cup water**

Place the strawberries in a large, heavy stainless-steel saucepan and crush them with a potato masher. Add the sugar, lemon juice, and water. Stirring often, bring to a boil over high heat. Lower the heat and simmer the strawberries for 10 minutes, until the sugar has dissolved. Turn the heat up high and, stirring occasionally, boil the mixture rapidly for 10 minutes. Skim off any white foam that may have accumulated on the surface. Cook rapidly for another 5 minutes. Remove from the heat and ladle the preserves into hot, clean 8-ounce jars. Cover with lids and cool.

YIELDS SIX OR SEVEN 8-OUNCE JARS

Broccoli frittata with saffron and lemon

Amazingly easy to prepare, and a wonderful addition to a brunch or a light lunch. The saffron adds a slightly exotic accent and gives the frittata its delightfully sunny look.

> 2 tablespoons olive oil
> 2 cups finely chopped onions
> 2 cups small broccoli florets
> 6 ounces fresh or smoked mozzarella cheese, cut into
> $^1/_2$-inch cubes
> 5 eggs
> $^1/_2$ cup heavy cream
> $^1/_2$ cup milk
> 1 teaspoon salt
> $^1/_2$ teaspoon crushed saffron
> $^1/_2$ teaspoon freshly ground black pepper
> $1^1/_2$ teaspoons grated lemon peel
> 2 tablespoons chopped fresh parsley
> $^1/_2$ cup freshly grated Parmesan cheese

Preheat the oven to 375°F. Butter a 10-by-$1^1/_2$-inch quiche dish or any low-sided ovenproof dish that will hold $4^3/_4$ cups of liquid.

Heat the oil in a heavy sauté pan. Add the onions and cook over medium heat for about 5 minutes, until the onions become transparent. Add the broccoli and sauté for 3 minutes longer, stirring the mixture a few times.

Transfer the vegetables to the prepared quiche dish. Scatter the mozzarella over the vegetables.

In a bowl, whisk together the eggs, cream, milk, salt, saffron, and pepper, until smooth. Pour the egg mixture over the vegetables. Sprinkle with the lemon peel, parsley, and Parmesan.

Bake for 35 to 40 minutes, or until the frittata has puffed and is nicely browned. Remove and let it rest for 10 minutes before serving.

Yields 4 to 6 servings

This can be made 1 day ahead of time, covered, and stored in the refrigerator. When ready to serve, uncover and reheat for 10 minutes in a preheated 375°F. oven. We often do this when we expect a large crowd for breakfast.

Vegetables such as leeks, red bell pepper, or fresh spinach can be substituted for the broccoli.

Mexican eggs with red sauce on flour tortillas

Inspired by the many great breakfasts that Detlef and I enjoyed while traveling through Mexico. If you're partial, as I am, to spicy dishes, this is it. Hot, spicy, or mild depends on how many jalapeño peppers you use. Or you can omit them altogether.

> *Four 8-inch flour tortillas*
> *3 cups finely chopped tomatoes*
> *3 garlic cloves, minced*
> *$^1/_2$ cup finely chopped onion*
> *2 jalapeño peppers, minced, with seeds*
> *$1^3/_4$ teaspoons salt*
> *$^1/_8$ teaspoon sugar*
> *$^1/_2$ cup finely chopped fresh cilantro, plus 16 cilantro leaves*
> *for garnish*
> *2 tablespoons butter*
> *$^1/_4$ cup water*
> *8 eggs, beaten*
> *2 cups grated sharp cheddar cheese*
> *1 cup sour cream*

Preheat the broiler to high.

In a 9-inch skillet, heat the tortillas until their surfaces blister. Transfer them to a baking sheet and set aside.

In a saucepan, combine the tomatoes, garlic, onion, jalapeños, $^1/_4$ teaspoon of the salt, the sugar, and chopped cilantro. Heat until just warm. Don't let the mixture boil or it will lose its fresh taste.

In a large skillet, melt the butter over low heat. Add the water and remaining salt to the beaten eggs and whisk until they're well blended. Pour the eggs into the heated skillet. Stir constantly but gently with a fork until the eggs are cooked to your liking.

Spread the sauce evenly over the 4 warm tortillas. Top each with the scrambled eggs. Sprinkle ½ cup of grated cheese over the eggs. Place the baking sheet with the tortillas under the broiler for 1 minute, or until the cheese melts.

Transfer the tortillas to 4 warm dinner plates. Top each with 1 teaspoon of sour cream. Garnish with the cilantro leaves, and serve the remaining sour cream on the side.

YIELDS 4 SERVINGS

Eggs baked in ramekins with parmesan cheese

Turn this into a festive meal by topping each ramekin with a spoonful of caviar just before serving along with warm slices of buttered toast.

2 tablespoons softened butter
6 tablespoons freshly grated Parmesan cheese
4 tablespoons heavy cream
8 eggs
4 teaspoons caviar (optional)

Preheat the oven to 400°F.

Butter the insides of 4 ramekins, 3 inches in diameter by 1³/₄ inches deep. Sprinkle the bottoms and sides of each with 1 tablespoon of the Parmesan. Spoon into each 1 tablespoon of cream. Break 2 eggs into each ramekin and sprinkle the tops with the remaining cheese. Bake for 16 minutes, making sure not to open the oven door during this time.

Remove from the oven and cool for 2 minutes. Top with caviar if desired, and serve.

YIELDS 4 SERVINGS

FOR THOSE WHO WANT THEIR
EGGS LESS RUNNY, ADD 3
MINUTES TO THE BAKING
TIME.

Blueberry muffins

These easy-to-make muffins filled with fresh, plump blueberries are a favorite at Loaves and Fishes and part of the continental breakfast that we serve at the Inn.

$2^1/_4$ cups flour
2 teaspoons baking powder
$^1/_2$ teaspoon baking soda
1 cup sugar
$^1/_4$ teaspoon salt
12 tablespoons ($1^1/_2$ sticks) melted butter, cooled slightly
Zest of 1 lemon, grated
1 teaspoon vanilla extract
2 eggs
$^3/_4$ cup milk
2 cups fresh blueberries

Preheat the oven to 375°F. Line 12 muffin cups with paper.

In a large bowl, combine the flour, baking powder, baking soda, sugar, salt, and butter. Add the lemon zest, vanilla, eggs, and milk. Beat by hand until the ingredients are well blended. Fold in the blueberries.

Scoop the batter into the muffin cups, filling each compartment level to the top. Bake for 25 to 30 minutes. To test for doneness, insert a toothpick into the center of the muffin. If it comes out clean, it's done.

YIELDS 12 MUFFINS

Lemon-blueberry cake

We serve this at breakfast and mid-afternoon with a tall glass of fresh lemonade topped with mint leaves from our garden.

2$^{1}/_{4}$ cups fresh blueberries
16 tablespoons (2 sticks) softened butter
1$^{1}/_{2}$ cups granulated sugar
Grated zest and juice of 2 lemons
3 eggs
3 cups flour
1 cup sour cream
1$^{1}/_{2}$ teaspoons baking soda

THE GLAZE

2 cups confectioners' sugar
$^{1}/_{2}$ cup fresh lemon juice

Preheat the oven to 350°F. Butter a 10-inch tube pan.

Spread the blueberries in 1 layer on a sheet pan and freeze for 1 hour. This will keep the berries from sinking to the bottom of the cake.

In a mixing bowl, beat together the butter, sugar, and lemon zest at high speed until light in color. Add the lemon juice, eggs, and 1 cup of the flour. Mix at medium speed until the batter is smooth and well blended. Add the sour cream, another cup of flour, and the baking soda. Mix at low speed until no traces of flour remain.

Combine the frozen blueberries with the remaining cup of flour. Fold this mixture into the batter, which should feel very thick.

Spoon the dough into the prepared tube pan. Bake for 1 hour, or until a toothpick inserted into the center comes out clean. Cool for 15 minutes in the pan.

To make the glaze, mix together the confectioners' sugar and lemon juice until smooth. Drizzle over the cake. Let the cake cool completely before removing it from its pan.

YIELDS 16 SLICES

FRESH LEMONADE

10 cups water
1 1/4 cups sugar
1 1/2 cups freshly squeezed
lemon juice
Ice cubes
6 fresh mint sprigs

COMBINE THE WATER AND SUGAR IN A PAN. SET OVER HIGH HEAT FOR 3 MINUTES, STIRRING, UNTIL THE SUGAR HAS DISSOLVED. REMOVE FROM THE HEAT, ADD THE LEMON JUICE, AND LET COOL SLIGHTLY. POUR THE LEMONADE OVER THE ICE CUBES PLACED IN 6 TALL GLASSES. GARNISH WITH MINT.

YIELDS 6 SERVINGS

Buttermilk scones

Just terrific with fresh preserves, crème fraîche (see box), and summer fruits.

> 2 cups flour
> $1/4$ cup sugar
> $1^{1}/_{2}$ teaspoons baking powder
> 12 tablespoons ($1^{1}/_{2}$ sticks) cold butter, cut into
>   pea-size pieces
> 2 eggs
> $1/2$ cup buttermilk

> EGG WASH

> 1 egg yolk
> 1 tablespoon milk
> 2 tablespoons sugar, for topping

Preheat the oven to 375°F. Butter a baking sheet.

In a large bowl, combine the flour, sugar, and baking powder. Mix in the butter with your hands until coarse crumbs form. Add the eggs and buttermilk. Stir the mixture with a fork until the dough pulls away from the sides of the bowl.

Turn the dough onto a countertop and knead until the dough just holds together. Roll out or pat the dough into a $1/2$-inch-thick rectangle. Cut into 12 triangles. Arrange the triangles on the baking sheet.

In a small bowl, beat together the egg yolk and milk and brush onto each scone. Sprinkle with sugar and bake for 20 to 25 minutes, or until golden brown.

YIELDS 12 SCONES

CRÈME FRAÎCHE

IN A SAUCEPAN, HEAT 2 CUPS HEAVY CREAM AND 2 TABLESPOONS BUTTERMILK UNTIL LUKEWARM. POUR INTO A CONTAINER WITH A TIGHT-FITTING LID AND SHAKE WELL. REMOVE THE LID AND LET THE CREAM STAND AT ROOM TEMPERATURE UNTIL IT SETS. THIS CAN TAKE ANYWHERE FROM 8 TO 24 HOURS. STORE IN THE REFRIGERATOR. THE CRÈME WILL KEEP FOR UP TO 4 WEEKS. YIELDS 2 CUPS

Danish almond breakfast braid

This delicious soft Danish loaf was always a must at our breakfast table at home. Like all yeast breads, it needs time for the dough to rise, but it is well worth the wait. Once it's made, it can be wrapped and frozen for up to 4 weeks.

1½ tablespoons dry yeast
¼ cup warm water (110°F.)
8 tablespoons (1 stick) warm melted butter
¾ cup sugar
1 cup milk
1 egg yolk
1 teaspoon almond extract
5 to 5½ cups flour
1½ teaspoons salt

THE TOPPING

1 egg yolk
1 tablespoon milk
¼ cup sugar
¼ cup sliced almonds

In a small bowl, combine the yeast and warm water and set it aside for 5 minutes to dissolve.

Pour the butter into the bowl of an electric mixer. Add the sugar, milk, egg yolk, almond extract, 2 cups of the flour and the softened yeast. Beat the mixture for about 8 minutes. Add 2 more cups of flour and the salt and mix 5 minutes longer. Scrape the dough onto a floured surface and knead, adding flour as you work, until the dough feels smooth and elastic. Place the dough in a lightly buttered bowl. Turn the dough once, then cover with a cloth and let rise in a warm place for about 2 hours.

Divide the dough in half. Divide each half into 3 equal pieces. Roll each piece into a 12-inch-long rope. Each set of 3 ropes should be braided with their ends tucked under.

Butter a baking sheet and dust with flour. Transfer the braided breads to the sheet.

For the topping, mix together the egg yolk and milk and brush this over each loaf. Sprinkle each loaf with sugar and almonds and let them rise in a warm place for 30 minutes.

Preheat the oven to 350°F.

Bake the breads for 35 to 40 minutes or until done. Tap the bottom of the loaves. If they sound hollow, they're done.

YIELDS 2 LOAVES

Salads
for spring and summer

....

> The discovery of a new dish does more for the
> happiness of mankind than the discovery of a star.

Brillat-Savarin

*S*alads have always challenged the imagination of even the most seasoned cooks, mainly because there are so many uses for salads and even more ways to create, dress, and present them. With a little ingenuity, you can adapt almost any combination of foods into a salad: meats, fish, vegetables, breads, nuts, grains, beans, pastas, fruits, and for some occasions, even a flower or two. Salads can be main dishes at brunches, lunches, picnics; side dishes before or after dinner; or even enjoyed as quick, pick-me-up snacks in the middle of the afternoon.

We compiled some of the most popular salads served to our guests at the Inn.

A few salads travel extremely well. When guests recently requested a picnic basket, we chose a combination of our three chicken salads, added *Potato Corn Salad* and *Marinated Broccoli Salad* and sent them off to the beach only to have them order the very same picnic lunch for the following day.

Salads offer even the novice cook opportunities to excel in the kitchen. The harmonies of taste, texture, color, and the endless assortment of foods with which one can experiment, open the door to a wealth of intriguing possibilities.

Croutons

I've included an easy recipe for homemade croutons because I believe they do much to enhance a simple salad of fresh spring and summer greens. My strongest suggestion is that you buy the very best olive oil and balsamic vinegar available. The lush fragrance of first-pressed olive oil means that a little of it will go a long way—and you cannot beat the taste.

> *1 loaf French bread, cut into $^1/_2$-inch cubes*
> *1 teaspoon salt*
> *2 garlic cloves*
> *$^1/_2$ cup olive oil*

Preheat the oven to 400°F.

Place the bread cubes in a bowl. In a separate bowl, mash the salt and garlic into a paste. Stir in the olive oil. Drizzle the garlic-oil over the bread cubes and blend well.

Place the cubes on a baking sheet and toast them in the oven for 10 minutes, or until golden brown. Cool. Store in an airtight container.

YIELDS 4 CUPS OR MORE, DEPENDING ON
THE SIZE OF THE LOAF OF BREAD.

Loaves and Fishes
grilled chicken salad

One of our most popular salads at Loaves and Fishes. And one of the recipes most sought after by our friends, guests, and loyal customers. So, here it is.

3 pounds chicken breasts, halved, skin, bones, and fat removed

THE MARINADE

1 tablespoon toasted sesame oil
1$^{1}/_{2}$ tablespoons soy sauce
Juice of $^{1}/_{2}$ lemon
$^{1}/_{2}$ teaspoon red pepper flakes
2 teaspoons Dijon mustard
$^{1}/_{4}$ cup dry white wine
1 large garlic clove, minced

THE DRESSING

1 garlic clove
1 tablespoon toasted sesame oil
2 tablespoons soy sauce
2 tablespoons sherry vinegar
$^{1}/_{3}$ cup olive oil

THE SALAD

$^{1}/_{2}$ cup thinly sliced red onion rings
1$^{1}/_{2}$ cups sugar snap peas
$^{1}/_{4}$ cup dry cranberries
$^{1}/_{2}$ teaspoon freshly ground black pepper
1 bunch fresh arugula leaves

(continued)

Place the chicken in a glass dish.

In a bowl, whisk together all the marinade ingredients and pour the marinade over the chicken. Marinate, covered, for at least 3 hours or overnight in the refrigerator.

Grill the chicken over hot coals or under a broiler, turning the pieces until just cooked through, 4 to 5 minutes per side. Discard the marinade. Cut the grilled chicken into bite-size strips and place them in a large bowl.

Using a food processor, puree the dressing ingredients until smooth. Pour the dressing over the chicken. Add the onion rings, snap peas, cranberries, and pepper. Toss to blend. Add the arugula and toss lightly.

YIELDS 6 SERVINGS

TO DOUBLE THIS RECIPE,
INCREASE BY HALF BOTH THE
MARINADE AND THE DRESSING
INGREDIENTS. IF YOU CAN'T
FIND DRIED CRANBERRIES,
USE DRIED CHERRIES.

Curried chicken salad

A wonderful blend of spicy, sweet, and crunchy. As a lunch, we serve it piled on a bed of salad greens. As a first course, we follow the salad with a pasta dish.

2 pounds chicken breasts, skin and bones removed
$^1/_2$ cup finely chopped celery
$^1/_2$ cup finely chopped bulb fennel
$^1/_3$ cup finely chopped onion
$^3/_4$ cup mayonnaise
$^3/_4$ cup finely chopped mango chutney
$^1/_3$ cup curry powder
2 tablespoons finely chopped fresh parsley

Place the chicken breasts in a large saucepan, cover with water, and bring to a boil. Simmer for 12 to 15 minutes, or until the chicken is just cooked. Drain, cover, and refrigerate for at least 1 hour.

Cut the chicken breasts into $^3/_4$-inch chunks and place them in a bowl. Add the rest of the ingredients and mix gently but thoroughly.

YIELDS 4 TO 6 SERVINGS

THIS SALAD IMPROVES OVER TIME, WHICH MEANS IT CAN BE PREPARED THE DAY BEFORE, COVERED, AND REFRIGERATED. IT WILL KEEP UP TO 3 DAYS WHEN STORED THIS WAY.

Smoked chicken salad

This takes just minutes to prepare and can be served for lunch, dinner, or on crusty rounds of bread at cocktail parties. Leftovers are just as tasty the next day. Try tucking sliced chicken breasts into sandwiches along with ripe avocados or with mozzarella cheese and tomatoes. Smoked chicken breasts can be found at most specialty food stores.

> 3 skinless and boneless smoked chicken breasts
> 1/2 cup toasted pine nuts
> 1/2 cup finely chopped onion
> 1 1/2 cups halved green grapes
> 1 cup finely chopped celery
> 1/2 cup finely chopped fresh parsley
> 2/3 cup mayonnaise
> 2 tablespoons fresh lemon juice
> 1 teaspoon salt
> 1 teaspoon freshly ground black pepper

Slice the chicken breasts into bite-size strips and place them in a bowl. Add the pine nuts, onion, grapes, celery, and parsley.

In a separate bowl, whisk together the mayonnaise, lemon juice, salt, and pepper. Pour the dressing over the chicken. Toss gently to blend.

YIELDS 6 SERVINGS

Fresh tuna salad

For a bit of variety, and a tasty treat, try using fresh halibut or bluefish instead of the tuna.

2 tablespoons olive oil
2$\frac{1}{2}$ pounds fresh tuna, cut into steaks 1 inch thick
$\frac{1}{4}$ cup distilled white vinegar
1 cup finely chopped red onions
1 cup finely chopped celery
$\frac{1}{4}$ cup drained capers
$\frac{1}{2}$ cup finely chopped fresh dill, loosely packed
$\frac{3}{4}$ cup mayonnaise
1 teaspoon salt
1 teaspoon freshly ground black pepper

Preheat the oven to 400°F.

Brush a sheet pan with a little of the olive oil. Brush the remaining olive oil on both sides of the tuna steaks. Place the steaks on the sheet pan and bake for 6 to 8 minutes. The tuna should be medium rare. Cool for 30 minutes, then cut the steaks into $\frac{1}{2}$-inch cubes.

Place the tuna in a bowl and sprinkle it with the vinegar, making sure all the pieces are covered. Add the rest of the ingredients and mix well.

YIELDS 4 TO 6 SERVINGS

Lobster salad

A luscious treat, and another of the most sought-after salads we've created at Loaves and Fishes.

> *1¼ pounds freshly cooked lobster meat*
> *½ cup mayonnaise*
> *1 teaspoon grated orange rind*
> *1 tablespoon fresh orange juice*
> *2 teaspoons fresh lemon juice*
> *½ teaspoon salt*
> *⅛ teaspoon freshly ground black pepper*
> *1 tablespoon drained capers*
> *4 cups mixed fresh salad greens*
> *1 tablespoon chopped dill (optional)*

Cut the lobster meat into bite-size pieces and place them in a bowl. Add the mayonnaise, orange rind, orange and lemon juices, salt, pepper, and capers. Toss gently to coat well.

Arrange 1 cup of salad greens on each of 4 plates. Scoop the lobster salad over the greens. Garnish with dill and serve.

YIELDS 4 SERVINGS

IF YOU WANT TO START
FROM SCRATCH, TWO
2-POUND LIVE LOBSTERS
COOKED FOR 15 TO 17
MINUTES WILL YIELD
APPROXIMATELY $1^{1}/_{4}$
POUNDS OF COOKED
LOBSTER MEAT. TO SAVE
TIME, I SUGGEST YOU BUY
FRESHLY COOKED LOBSTER
MEAT FROM YOUR
FISHMONGER.

Potato corn salad

There seems to be as many potato salad recipes as there are cooks. Excellent as a summer dinner salad or for picnics in the garden. It goes so well with grilled chicken, meats, or sausages.

> *2 pounds small Yukon Gold new potatoes*
> *3 ears of corn*
> *1/3 cup hot chicken stock (page 84)*
> *3/4 cup finely chopped fresh chives or scallions*
> *3/4 cup finely chopped fresh curly parsley*
> *1 teaspoon salt*
> *1/2 teaspoon freshly ground black pepper*
> *2 tablespoons tarragon vinegar*
> *6 tablespoons olive oil*
> *2 teaspoons Dijon mustard*
> *6 sprigs fresh tarragon for garnish*

Place the potatoes in a large saucepan, cover with water, and bring to a boil. Lower the heat and simmer for 15 minutes, or until the potatoes are just tender. Drain and let cool.

Bring a large pot of water to a boil, add the corn, and boil for 5 minutes. Using tongs, transfer the ears of corn to a plate to cool.

Cut the potatoes into bite-size pieces and place them in a salad bowl. Pour the hot chicken stock over the potatoes.

Using a knife in a downward motion, remove the corn kernels from the cob and add them to the salad bowl. Add the chives, parsley, salt, and pepper.

Combine the tarragon vinegar, olive oil, and mustard in a small container with a tight-fitting lid. Shake well. Pour the dressing over the salad and toss to blend. Serve at room temperature, garnished with fresh tarragon.

To make a fall potato salad, leave out the corn and increase the amount of potatoes to 3 pounds. Add a ripe pear cut into bite-size pieces and $\frac{1}{2}$ pound crumbled Roquefort cheese, and substitute red wine vinegar for the tarragon vinegar. Serve on a bed of arugula leaves.

Panzanella

My own version of the delicious Italian bread salad. This melange of crunchy garden fresh vegetables tossed in a tasty vinaigrette is in demand all summer long.

1 small loaf French bread (about 6 cups), cut into 1-inch chunks
3 tablespoons olive oil
1 red bell pepper, stemmed, cored, and cut into chunks
1 yellow bell pepper, stemmed, cored, and cut into chunks
1 green bell pepper, stemmed, cored, and cut into chunks
1½ cups seeded cucumber chunks
1 cup thinly sliced red onions
2 cups ripe summer tomato chunks

THE VINAIGRETTE

1 garlic clove, crushed
3 tablespoons red wine vinegar
½ cup olive oil
¼ teaspoon salt
¼ teaspoon sugar
¼ teaspoon freshly ground black pepper

Preheat the oven to 400°F.

Place the bread cubes in a bowl, sprinkle them with the olive oil, and toss to coat. Arrange the cubes in 1 layer on a baking sheet. Bake for 8 to 10 minutes, or until golden brown. Set aside to cool.

Place all the vegetables in a large bowl. Add the toasted bread chunks. Combine the vinaigrette ingredients in a jar with a tight-fitting lid and shake well. Pour the dressing over the vegetables and bread. Mix well. Serve at room temperature.

YIELDS 6 SERVINGS

Marinated broccoli salad

For a perfect summer lunch, add chunks of vine-ripened tomatoes, toss in some rich black olives, and, for the final touch, crumble fresh feta cheese over the top.

1 small head of broccoli, trimmed and cut into small florets

$1/2$ pound small sugar snap peas

1 cup coarsely chopped radicchio

2 tablespoons red wine vinegar

$1/3$ cup good-quality olive oil

1 small garlic clove, minced

1 teaspoon finely chopped fresh oregano

1 teaspoon salt

$1/2$ teaspoon freshly ground black pepper

Place the broccoli florets, sugar snap peas, and radicchio in a salad bowl.

Combine the remaining ingredients in a small saucepan. Heat over medium flame until the garlic starts to sizzle. Don't let the garlic brown or the liquid come to a boil.

Pour the hot dressing over the vegetables and toss well to coat. Refrigerate for 6 to 24 hours. Serve at room temperature.

YIELDS 6 SERVINGS

Pea shoots
and sugar snap peas

My grandchildren love to eat freshly picked sugar snap peas as they come off the vine. Me, too.

$1/3$ pound (8 cups loosely packed) pea shoots
$3/4$ pound sugar snap peas, strings removed

The dressing

1 tablespoon rice vinegar
1 tablespoon toasted sesame oil
2 teaspoons light brown sugar
2 teaspoons soy sauce
$1/2$ teaspoon salt

Cut the pea shoots into 3-inch pieces and place them in a salad bowl along with the sugar snap peas.

Combine the dressing ingredients in a container with a tight-fitting lid and shake well. Pour over the salad and toss to coat well.

Yields 4 servings

THIS SALAD SHOULD BE
SERVED IMMEDIATELY
SINCE THE DRESSING TENDS
TO WILT THE PEA LEAVES IF
LEFT TOO LONG. FRESH PEA
SHOOTS, ALTHOUGH
RELATIVELY NEW TO OUR
KITCHENS, ARE WIDELY
AVAILABLE FROM EARLY
SPRING THROUGH
MOST OF THE SUMMER.

Spinach salad

❦

Fresh peaches and toasted pecans give this salad just the right amount of natural sweetness and crunchy texture. We often serve it after our main course, with some fresh goat cheese or English Stilton on the side.

> **2 bunches flat-leaf spinach, stems removed**
> **$^1/_3$ cup thinly sliced red onion rings**
> **2 ripe peaches, halved, pitted, and sliced**
> **$^1/_2$ cup toasted pecan halves**
> **2 tablespoons red wine vinegar**
> **$^1/_3$ cup olive oil**
> **1 teaspoon Dijon mustard**
> **1 teaspoon salt**
> **$^1/_2$ teaspoon freshly ground black pepper**

Place the spinach leaves in a salad bowl. Add the onion rings, peaches, and pecans.

Combine the vinegar, olive oil, mustard, salt, and pepper in a container with a tight-fitting lid; shake well. Pour over the salad. Toss lightly and serve.

❦

Yields 4 to 6 servings

Black beans with coriander

A hearty salad that is great with grilled chicken. The cooked beans keep nicely for up to 3 days in the refrigerator, which turns this into one of those handy do-ahead salads. Once the beans are cooked, the rest is amazingly simple.

2 cups dried black beans
$1/4$ cup olive oil
$1/4$ cup sherry vinegar
1 cup thinly sliced onions
3 medium tomatoes, finely chopped
2 ripe avocados, peeled, pitted, and cut into small pieces
$1/8$ teaspoon cayenne
1 teaspoon ground cumin
2 teaspoons salt
1 cup chopped fresh coriander leaves

Soak the beans overnight in enough cold water so that you have 3 inches of water to spare at the top. The next day, cook the beans in the soaking water for 45 minutes to 1 hour, until done. Drain and place the beans in a bowl.

Pour the olive oil and vinegar over the hot beans. Mix gently and let cool to room temperature. When cool, add the rest of the ingredients. Mix gently and serve.

YIELDS 6 SERVINGS

PUREE ANY LEFTOVER BEANS MEDIUM FINE. SHAPE INTO CAKES. SAUTÉ IN 1 TABLESPOON PEANUT OIL, AND SERVE WITH A GREEN SALAD. THEY'RE FABULOUS.

Cucumber salad

2 seedless cucumbers, each about 10 inches in length
1½ teaspoons salt
½ teaspoon freshly ground black pepper
½ cup distilled white vinegar
1 tablespoon sugar
2 tablespoons finely chopped fresh dill

Thinly slice the cucumbers. Place them in a bowl. Add the rest of the ingredients and toss well.

YIELDS 4 SERVINGS

Tomato, mint, and parsley salad

Our version of fatoush, this is an easy-to-make Mediterranean bread salad that should be served only during the summer—mainly because it requires the ripest, sweetest tomatoes; young parsley leaves; and fresh, fragrant mint.

One 8-inch pita bread, brushed with 1 tablespoon olive oil

THE SALAD

3 cups tomatoes, chopped into 1-inch chunks
2 cups cucumbers that have been split lengthwise, seeded and cut into
 1-inch chunks
4 cups curly parsley, loosely packed, with stems removed
2 cups mint leaves, loosely packed
1 lemon, sliced paper thin
1 tablespoon fresh lemon juice
2 tablespoons best-quality olive oil
1 teaspoon salt

Preheat the oven to 400°F.

Cut the pita bread into 12 small wedges. Arrange them on a baking sheet. Bake for 10 minutes, or until the wedges are crisp and lightly browned. Cool.

Combine all the salad ingredients in a large bowl. Add the pita crisps and toss well.

YIELDS 4 TO 6 SERVINGS

Starters
for spring and summer

Since we first opened our doors, the Inn has become a place where people congregate for all manner of celebrations: cocktail parties, dinner parties, weddings, birthdays, anniversaries, and bar mitzvahs, to mention just a few.

Miraculously, the weather has, for the most part, favored us with perfect days, which means the living-room doors remain wide open and people are able to wander in and out, munching on hors d'oeuvre, refilling their glasses with wine or champagne, meeting up with relatives or friends. When the weather turns obstinately perverse, we erect a marquee in the garden where the party guests can carry on with their festivities. With music drowning out the sound of rain, fresh flowers galore, and lots of candlelight, the large white tent seems to add a magical charm and coziness to these gatherings.

Hors d'oeuvre, canapés, and dips are the words that customarily describe the fare offered at cocktail parties. At Loaves and Fishes we refer to these foods as "starters." For us, that seems to better characterize this assortment of multifaceted offerings. Homemade gravlax, for instance, is extremely versatile. Offered thinly sliced, with chopped onion and capers, garnished with sprigs of fresh dill, it becomes a gorgeous introduction to an elegant dinner. It can also be served on grainy bread for a late after-theater gathering. As an hors d'oeuvre, it can be piled onto cucumber rounds, stuffed in hulled-out cherry tomatoes, served on toast with a dab of crème fraîche, or on the usual squares of dark or grainy bread. Homemade gravlax is the best. It takes very little time to prepare and kindly does its own work, marinating in the refrigerator while you go about preparing your party. It lasts for days, and leftovers, if there are any, can be chopped by hand and transformed into a gorgeous salmon tartare. Just sprinkle it with a little fresh lemon and fold it onto tiny squares of toasted bread and you have another wonderful "starter" to serve with your drinks.

A plate of assorted starters, such as our Cucumber, Egg, and Caviar; or Shrimp, Horseradish, and Arugula; and Baba Ghanouj, nestled in cradles of radicchio leaves, serves as a wonderful first course. Individually, with their distinctive colors, delectable flavors, and variety of textures, they are welcome offerings at buffets and cocktail parties.

Many of the following recipes can and should be made in advance. When planning a party, I strongly urge that you read over each recipe, make sure you have all the essentials at hand, and try to have the starters, salads, and desserts ready and waiting before your guests arrive. This will leave you time to concentrate more effectively on your main course, and, more importantly, it will give you time to relax and enjoy your own party.

A cucumber should be well sliced, and dressed with pepper and vinegar, and then thrown out, as good for nothing.

SAMUEL JOHNSON

Gravlax
with mustard sauce

This is marinated salmon at its best. For a first course, offer 2 or 3 thin slices of gravlax on a dinner plate, fill half a scooped-out lemon with mustard sauce, and add that to the plate along with toasted grainy-bread triangles. A sprig of fresh dill adds both color and bouquet.

1 side of salmon (2^{1}/$_{2}$ pounds), all bones removed, skin left on
^{1}/$_{3}$ cup salt
^{1}/$_{4}$ cup sugar
^{1}/$_{4}$ cup freshly ground black pepper
4 cups coarsely chopped fresh dill
^{1}/$_{4}$ cup vodka or brandy

THE SAUCE

^{1}/$_{4}$ cup honey
^{3}/$_{4}$ cup Dijon mustard
1 tablespoon fresh lemon juice
^{1}/$_{4}$ teaspoon freshly ground black pepper

Place the salmon in a shallow noncorrosive pan. In a small bowl, combine the salt, sugar, and pepper. Rub the mixture gently onto the salmon, cover it with the chopped dill, and sprinkle the top with vodka or brandy. Fold the salmon in half. Wrap it in plastic wrap, weigh it down with a brick or heavy cans, and refrigerate it for at least 3 days, or up to a week, turning the fish once each day. The salmon should be served thinly sliced.

To make the sauce, combine all the ingredients in a small bowl and mix well. Serve on the side.

FOR A DIFFERENT TASTE, TRY
USING MINT LEAVES OR
CORIANDER LEAVES IN PLACE
OF THE DILL.

Cucumber, egg, and caviar

An easy-to-make yet elegant hors d'oeuvre, which we serve at cocktail parties or before dinner with a glass of chilled champagne.

> *1 seedless cucumber*
> *3 eggs, hard boiled*
> *$^1/_2$ cup sour cream*
> *1 tablespoon finely chopped fresh chives*
> *4 ounces salmon caviar, or other caviar of your choice*

Cut the cucumber into twelve $^1/_4$-inch-thick slices. Cut each egg into 4 slices, saving the ends for another use.

Combine the sour cream and chives in a bowl. Arrange the cucumber slices on a tray lined with linen napkins. Top each cucumber round with a slice of egg. Dab each egg with sour cream–chive mixture, then carefully spoon caviar on top of the sour cream.

YIELDS 12 PIECES

Baba ghanouj
on endive leaves

Even though you can serve this deliciously soft and savory spread on toasted pita bread triangles, the endive seems to have been built exactly for the job: sturdy, tasty, and shaped just right.

2 small eggplants, total weight 2 pounds
2¹/₂ tablespoons fresh lemon juice
2 garlic cloves, minced
3 tablespoons sesame tahini
2 teaspoons olive oil
1 teaspoon salt
¹/₂ teaspoon freshly ground black pepper
3 tablespoons finely chopped fresh parsley
16 whole endive leaves
16 small sprigs of watercress

Preheat the oven to 425°F.

Place the eggplants in a small roasting pan and bake for 35 to 40 minutes, until they're soft. Remove from the pan and, when cool enough to handle, cut the eggplants in half. Scrape out the insides, discarding the skin.

Place the pulp in the bowl of a food processor. Add the lemon juice, garlic, tahini, olive oil, salt, and pepper. Puree until smooth. Transfer to another bowl.

Arrange the endive leaves on a serving platter. Spoon 1 heaping teaspoon of baba ghanouj onto each leaf. Top with a sprig of watercress and serve.

YIELDS 16 HORS D'OEUVRE

Caviar dip

We make masses of this delicious dip at Loaves and Fishes throughout the summer months. At the Inn, we serve it surrounded by strips of toast, endive leaves, and broccoli florets for scooping.

> *²/₃ cup sour cream*
> *¹/₃ cup mayonnaise*
> *¹/₄ cup salmon roe (large roe type)*
> *¹/₄ cup finely chopped scallion greens*
> *¹/₈ teaspoon Tabasco sauce*
> *¹/₄ teaspoon salt*

In a small bowl, combine the sour cream and mayonnaise. Gently fold in the rest of the ingredients. Chill the dip until ready to serve. This can be made up to 3 days ahead of time.

YIELDS 1¹/₄ CUPS

Parsley, basil, and caper sauce

A versatile sauce that has a special zing. A great dip for raw vegetables, an excellent sauce for chicken and shrimp, or pour it over your favorite pasta. Hot or cold, as a sauce or a dip, it's delicious.

> 3 cups curly parsley leaves, packed
> 1$\frac{1}{2}$ cups basil leaves, packed
> 8 anchovy fillets
> 2 tablespoons drained capers
> 2 garlic cloves, finely chopped
> 2 tablespoons Dijon mustard
> 1 teaspoon salt
> $\frac{1}{8}$ teaspoon cayenne
> 1$\frac{1}{2}$ cups good-quality olive oil

Place all the ingredients in a blender and puree until they're smooth. You may find you have to do this in 2 batches.

YIELDS 2 CUPS

Radish and fresh goat cheese canapés

4 ounces fresh goat cheese
1 bunch radishes
2 tablespoons finely chopped onion
2 tablespoons finely chopped fresh parsley
$1/8$ teaspoon cayenne
$3/4$ teaspoon salt
2 tablespoons extra-virgin olive oil
1 tablespoon milk (if needed)
3 large slices sourdough bread

Place the goat cheese in a shallow bowl. Finely chop enough radishes to make $1/3$ cup. Add the chopped radishes, onion, parsley, cayenne, salt, and olive oil to the goat cheese. Using a fork, mash the ingredients together until the mixture becomes creamy and holds its shape. If it seems dry, add 1 tablespoon of milk.

Divide the spread evenly over the bread slices, covering them completely. Cut each slice into 6 pieces. Thinly slice the remaining radishes and top each canapé with 3 or 4 radish rounds.

YIELDS 18 PIECES

Bruschetta with summer tomatoes and basil

A simple and thoroughly delicious salad made with sweet, garden-grown tomatoes, warmed by the sun.

$^1/_3$ *cup olive oil*
1 large garlic clove, peeled, split lengthwise
16 slices French bread, $^3/_4$ inch thick

THE TOPPING

1$^1/_2$ pounds ripe tomatoes, finely chopped
$^1/_2$ *cup finely chopped red onion*
$^1/_3$ *cup pitted and finely chopped black olives*
1 tablespoon olive oil
1 teaspoon salt
$^1/_2$ *teaspoon freshly ground black pepper*
12 fresh basil leaves, cut into fine julienne

Preheat the broiler for 10 minutes.

In a small pan, warm the oil and garlic over medium heat for 5 minutes. Brush the garlic oil over both sides of the bread slices. Arrange the slices on a sheet pan. Toast each side under the broiler until lightly brown.

Combine all the topping ingredients in a bowl. Mound the tomato mixture on the toasted bread and serve.

YIELDS 16 HORS D'OEUVRE

Roasted green asparagus with prosciutto and parmesan

1¹/₂ pounds green asparagus
¹/₄ cup olive oil
1 tablespoon kosher salt
1 tablespoon fresh lemon juice
¹/₄ pound sliced prosciutto, cut into strips
¹/₄ cup freshly grated Parmesan cheese

Preheat the oven to 450°F.

Peel the asparagus with a vegetable peeler. Cut off and discard the tough ends. Place the spears in a single layer on a baking sheet. Sprinkle with the olive oil and salt. Roast for 10 to 12 minutes, or until done to your liking. Remove from the oven and sprinkle with the lemon juice.

Divide the spears equally onto 4 plates. Add equal amounts of prosciutto to each plate, and sprinkle with the Parmesan cheese. Serve warm.

YIELDS 4 SERVINGS AS A FIRST COURSE

Shrimp, horseradish, and arugula on rye toast

3/4 cup cream cheese
3/4 cup crème fraîche or sour cream
1 teaspoon Dijon mustard
1/4 cup drained prepared horseradish
1/2 teaspoon salt
Twelve 2-inch rounds rye toast
12 arugula leaves
12 medium shrimp (about 3/4 pound), cooked and shelled

In a food processor, combine the cream cheese, crème fraîche, mustard, horseradish, and salt. Puree until they're smooth. Scrape into a bowl and set aside.

Coat each toast round with 1 teaspoon of horseradish spread. Place 1 arugula leaf on top of each round. Add 1 more teaspoon of spread and crown each round with 1 shrimp.

YIELDS 12 HORS D'OEUVRE

Rye bread

A hearty loaf that is fabulous when served hot from the oven. Thick slices are great with a bowl of soup, or, thinly sliced, the bread is wonderful with spreads or starters.

> *2 cups warm water (about 110°F.)*
> *¹/₄ cup dark brown sugar*
> *2 tablespoons dry yeast*
> *3 cups unbleached flour*
> *2¹/₂ cups coarsely ground rye flour*
> *³/₄ cup rye flakes*
> *1 cup whole-wheat bran*
> *2 tablespoons salt*
> *¹/₄ cup safflower oil*
> *1 egg yolk*
> *1 tablespoon cream*

Pour the warm water into the bowl of an electric mixer fitted with a dough hook. Add the sugar and yeast and let the mixture stand for about 5 minutes for the yeast to soften. Then add 2 cups of unbleached flour and the rye flour. With the dough hook in place, mix the batter for 8 minutes. Add the rye flakes, bran, salt, and safflower oil. Mix again for 6 minutes.

Scrape the dough onto a lightly floured work surface and knead, adding the remaining cup of unbleached flour to keep it from sticking. Place the dough in a buttered bowl. Cover with a cloth and let the dough rise in a warm place for about 45 minutes, until the dough has doubled in size.

Preheat the oven to 350°F. Divide the dough in half. Roll each half into a ball and place them on a flour-dusted baking sheet.

In a small bowl, beat together the egg yolk and cream until smooth. Brush the mixture over the top of each loaf. Cut a few slits, about ¹/₂ inch deep, into the top of each loaf. Let the breads rise in a warm place for about 30 minutes or until doubled in size. Place in the center of the oven and bake for 35 to 40 minutes. Remove from oven. Tap the bottom of each loaf. If they sound hollow, the bread is done.

When cool, cover well in plastic wrap and store at room temperature. The bread will keep for up to 3 days although it is best consumed the day it has been baked.

YIELDS 2 LOAVES

Shrimp with lemon and fresh thyme

A simple and savory dish that can be prepared a day ahead. We serve it either as a first course or as an hors d'oeuvre with a basket of freshly baked garlic toast on the side.

4 quarts water
9 sprigs fresh thyme
$1/2$ lemon, cut into 4 pieces
2 dozen large shrimp in their shells
4 ripe plum tomatoes, peeled, seeded, cut into $1/4$-inch-wide strips
3 celery ribs, cut into $1/4$-by-2-inch-wide strips
1 red onion, peeled, cut into paper-thin rings
2 lemons, cut into paper-thin slices
2 tablespoons fresh lemon juice
$1/3$ cup olive oil
1 tablespoon whole fresh thyme leaves

THE GARLIC TOAST

1 loaf French bread
8 tablespoons (1 stick) softened butter
2 garlic cloves
1 teaspoon kosher salt
1 tablespoon finely chopped fresh parsley

In a large pot, bring the water to a boil. Add 1 sprig of fresh thyme, the lemon pieces, and the shrimp and bring to another boil. The shrimp will be done at the boiling point. Remove from the heat and drain.

When the shrimp are cool enough to handle, remove their shells. Place the shrimp in a bowl. Add the tomatoes, celery, red onion, and lemon slices. Sprinkle with the lemon juice, olive oil, and thyme leaves. Toss well to blend. Refrigerate for at least 1 hour or up to 24 hours before serving.

Preheat the oven to 400°F.

To make the garlic toast, cut 4 thick slices of French bread on the diagonal so you get long oval slices. In a bowl, mash the butter, garlic, salt, and parsley together until you have a paste. Spread the mixture on the bread and place the slices on a sheet pan. Toast the bread in the hot oven for 8 to 10 minutes, or until the slices are light brown.

To serve, divide the shrimp among 4 plates. Garnish with the remaining thyme sprigs, and serve with the garlic toast on the side.

YIELDS 4 SERVINGS

spring and summer

Soups

....

Many people associate soup with colder weather, but summer soups, which can often be served either hot or cold, are also truly wondrous. Some people are daunted by soup recipes. Don't be. Made from fresh, seasonal fruits and vegetables, they can be whipped up in no time. All you need to do is follow a few simple and basic rules: Heat a bit of olive oil in which you sauté onions, then add the fresh vegetables or fruits of your choice and some homemade stock and let it all simmer for twenty minutes before pureeing.

One of the fundamentals of a good soup is to use good stock. Never use water, since it will add nothing to the soup's body, taste, or nourishment. I have included simple stock recipes that can be prepared easily and stored in your freezer. Stocks are essential—the fundamental ingredient in almost all gravies, sauces, and, of course, soups, summer and winter.

The beauty of these soups is their flexibility. They can be made up to three days before your dinner party and sit in the refrigerator until moments before your guests arrive. Most of these recipes can be expanded for larger dinner parties by simply doubling the ingredients. And, even though they were created as chilled soups, most of the recipes can—if the weather suddenly turns nasty—be served hot without compromising their taste or quality.

These soups were conceived as first courses, however, they are also especially refreshing when served with sandwiches, as a light lunch on long, hot summer days.

Remember, soups created with the freshest possible produce become truly exemplary. And their glorious colors floating in pretty bowls will never fail to brighten the start of a festive meal.

*Early produce is never as good as produce
in season, and the pleasure of eating something because it is expensive
has nothing to do with the taste of good cuisine.*

X. MARCEL BOULESTIN
FRENCH CHEF, 1878–1943

Fish stock

Never throw away shrimp shells. Freeze them and save them for this stock. They really enhance the flavor.

> 6 pounds fish bones from white lean fish only
> Any shrimp shells available
> 3 cups white wine
> 1 large onion, peeled and quartered
> 1 fennel bulb, cut into quarters
> 2 carrots, cut into large pieces
> 2 bay leaves
> 10 parsley sprigs
> 2 garlic cloves, peeled and crushed
> 4 fresh thyme sprigs
> 10 black peppercorns
> 4 quarts water

Place all the ingredients in a large stockpot. Bring to a boil. Lower the heat and simmer gently, uncovered, for 30 minutes. Strain into a large bowl. Chill.

Store in 2-cup containers in either the refrigerator or the freezer to use as needed. Remember to label the containers. Certain stocks do tend to look alike. When refrigerated, the stock will keep for 4 to 5 days. Frozen, it can last up to 3 months. Deep frozen, it can last up to 1 year.

YIELDS APPROXIMATELY 3½ QUARTS
(14 CUPS)

Rich chicken stock

To make a really flavorful, strong stock, use lots of neck and backbones or whole chickens or, any combination of the two.

> 4 pounds chicken bones
> One 3-pound chicken
> 4 large onions, peeled and quartered
> 2 large carrots, cut into 1-inch lengths
> 2 bay leaves
> 4 celery ribs with leaves, cut into 3-inch lengths
> 12 black peppercorns
> 12 sprigs parsley
> 6 sprigs fresh thyme
> 2 large bay leaves

Place all the ingredients in a large stockpot. Cover with cold water to come 4 inches above the chicken, and bring to a boil. Lower the heat, partially cover the pot, and leave the stock to simmer gently for 3 hours.

Strain into a large bowl, discarding the solids. Chill the stock. Skim the fat off the top and ladle into 2-cup containers. Store in the refrigerator or freezer to use as needed.

I suggest you label each container with the contents and preparation date. It will last up to 3 months in the freezer.

YIELDS APPROXIMATELY 3 QUARTS
(12 CUPS)

(continued)

Swedish Pancakes with Warm Blueberry Sauce

Lobster Cakes on Schnusch with Tarragon-Chive Sauce

Grilled Leg of Spring Lamb
Oven-Roasted Potatoes with Fresh Rosemary
Pea Shoots and Sugar Snap Peas
Rhubarb Compote

Rhubarb-Blackberry Crisp in Small Ramekins on Stand
Chocolate Tartlets with Black Cherries and Espresso Crème Anglaise
Strawberry Meringue Torte

FOR A CHANGE OF FLAVOR,
ADD THE PEEL OF 1 LEMON
AFTER THE CELERY, AND 2
TABLESPOONS CHOPPED
FRESH GINGER. AFTER THE
STOCK IS DONE, ADD 2
TABLESPOONS SOY SAUCE
AND 1 TABLESPOON RICE
VINEGAR. USE AS YOU
WOULD REGULAR STOCK.

Brown veal stock

2 tablespoons olive oil
6 pounds veal leg bones
12 cups water
2 large Spanish onions, peeled and cut into quarters
1 large carrot, cut into 4 pieces
2 bay leaves
10 sprigs parsley
2 sprigs fresh rosemary
15 black peppercorns

Preheat the oven to 450°F.

Pour the olive oil into a large roasting pan. Add the veal bones in one layer and roast them for 1 hour. Transfer the bones to a stockpot. Pour 2 cups of the water into the roasting pan and set it over high heat. Cook long enough to scrape up all of the brown bits from the bottom of the pan. This will add flavor to the stock.

Pour the browned stock into the stockpot with the veal bones. Add the remaining ingredients. Bring to a boil. Lower the heat, cover, and simmer for 1½ hours. Uncover and simmer for 1 hour longer to reduce the liquid by half.

Discard the bones and strain the stock into a large bowl. Cool. Pour into 1-cup containers and refrigerate or freeze to use as needed. When refrigerated, stock will keep for 4 to 5 days. Frozen, it can last up to 3 months. Deep-frozen, it will last up to 1 year.

YIELDS 4 TO 5 CUPS

Watercress and potato soup

Light yet fortifying, this soup can be served hot or chilled.

> 4 tablespoons (¹/₂ stick) butter
> 3 cups chopped onions
> ³/₄ pound potatoes, peeled and cut into 1-inch pieces (2 cups)
> 7 cups chicken stock (page 84)
> 2 teaspoons salt
> ¹/₂ teaspoon ground white pepper
> 1 bunch watercress with stems, cut into 2-inch pieces, plus
>   6 whole sprigs watercress for garnish

In a large saucepan, sauté the butter and onions for 10 minutes over low heat until the onions become glossy. Do not brown them. Add the potatoes, chicken stock, salt, and pepper. Raise the heat and bring to a boil. Lower the heat, cover, and simmer for 35 minutes. Add the watercress pieces and cook, uncovered, for 2 minutes longer. Remove from the heat and set aside to cool.

After it has cooled, puree the soup in a blender. You will have to do this in batches. Serve ice cold or very hot, garnished with sprigs of watercress.

YIELDS 5 OR 6 SERVINGS

AS YOU CAN SEE, THIS SOUP IS
A BREEZE TO MAKE. IT CAN BE
PREPARED UP TO 3 DAYS
AHEAD OF TIME AND KEPT
COVERED IN THE
REFRIGERATOR UNTIL NEEDED.

Summer borscht

A guest at the Inn told me this was the best borscht he'd ever had; a wonderful compliment since his mother came from Russia and he lives in New York City where one can find all sorts of borschts. I love this soup too. It has deliciously vivid color that matches its taste. We serve it chilled, with a basket of Caraway Breadsticks (page 90) on the side.

2 pounds fresh small beets, greens removed
1¹/2 cups beet cooking liquid
2 cups Rich Chicken Stock (page 84)
1¹/2 cups sour cream
¹/2 cup plain yogurt
1 teaspoon rice vinegar
1¹/2 teaspoons salt
1 teaspoon freshly ground black pepper
2 cups finely chopped seedless cucumbers
¹/2 cup chopped scallions
2 tablespoons chopped parsley
2 tablespoons chopped fresh dill, plus fresh dill sprigs
for garnish

Place the unpeeled beets in a saucepan, cover with water, and bring to a boil. Lower the heat and simmer, covered, until the beets are just tender. This should take 30 to 40 minutes, depending on the size of the beets. Using a slotted spoon, remove the beets and cool. Strain the cooking liquid through cheesecloth and reserve it until cold.

In a large bowl, combine 1$\frac{1}{2}$ cups of the cooled beet liquid with the chicken stock, sour cream, yogurt, vinegar, salt, and pepper. Using a wire whisk, beat the mixture until smooth and creamy. Peel the beets and cut them into small slices. Add the beets to the soup mixture along with the cucumbers, scallions, parsley, and chopped dill. Chill the soup for at least 3 hours or overnight.

Serve chilled, in deep soup plates, garnished with sprigs of fresh dill.

YIELDS 6 SERVINGS

Caraway breadsticks

1 cup warm water (about 110°F)
2 teaspoons dry yeast
2 teaspoons sugar
4 cups all-purpose flour
3¹/₂ teaspoons salt
3 tablespoons caraway seeds
1 egg white beaten with 1 tablespoon water

In a bowl, combine the warm water, yeast, and sugar. Stir once and let stand for 5 minutes until the yeast is dissolved. Add 2 cups of the flour and 1¹/₂ teaspoons of the salt. Beat the mixture vigorously, with wooden spoon or mixer. Add 1 more cup of flour and beat until smooth.

Turn the dough onto a lightly floured surface. Knead the dough, adding the remaining flour, until the dough is smooth and elastic, about 8 minutes. Return the ball of dough to the bowl, cover it with a kitchen towel, and place it in a warm area to rise for 45 minutes, or until doubled in size.

Preheat the oven to 375°F. Butter two 13-by-18-inch breadstick pans.

Turn the dough onto a floured work surface, divide it into 30 equal pieces, and roll each piece into a 13-inch-long rope. Sprinkle the remaining 2 teaspoons salt and caraway seeds on the work table. Roll each bread rope a few times back and forth. Place the ropes on the breadstick pans.

Brush the beaten egg white and water over the breadsticks. Let them stand in a warm place for 15 minutes, or until they've doubled in size. Bake for 15 to 20 minutes, until the breadsticks are evenly and lightly browned.

YIELDS 30 BREADSTICKS

The breadsticks can be made a day ahead and reheated in a 375°F oven for 8 minutes. We use perforated pans to get added crispness and serve these delicious breadsticks hot or at room temperature.

Tomato, carrot, and orange soup

On blustery spring nights, we serve this richly satisfying soup hot, and, on hot summer days, we serve it chilled. Sprinkle the soup with fresh basil leaves, and serve it with baked pita bread triangles spread with a little pesto. Delicious!

> 4 tablespoons (^{1}/$_2$ stick) butter
> 2^1/$_2$ cups chopped onions
> 1 cup chopped carrots
> 1 teaspoon grated orange rind
> ^{1}/$_8$ teaspoon ground cloves
> 1^1/$_2$ cups fresh orange juice
> 6 cups (two 28-ounce cans) Italian plum tomatoes with
>   their juices
> 1^1/$_2$ teaspoons salt
> ^{1}/$_2$ teaspoon freshly ground white pepper

In a large soup pot, melt the butter. Sauté the onions over very low heat for 10 minutes, until they turn glossy. Do not let them brown. Add the rest of the ingredients and bring the mixture to a boil. Lower the heat, cover, and simmer for 30 minutes. Cool to room temperature.

When cool, puree the soup in a blender in batches. Chill.

YIELDS 6 SERVINGS

WE FIND THAT CANNED ITALIAN PLUM TOMATOES ARE EXCELLENT TO USE IN THIS RECIPE. WHEN WE TRY FRESH TOMATOES, WE WIND UP WITH A DIFFERENT SOUP EACH TIME. HOWEVER, IF YOU WOULD LIKE TO USE FRESH TOMATOES, USE 6 CUPS. YOU WILL END UP WITH THE SAME QUANTITY WHEN FINISHED.

Garden fresh pea soup

Chilled or hot, this soup not only tastes deliciously sweet and fresh, but its color adds great vibrancy to your table.

> 2 tablespoons butter
> 2 tablespoons olive oil
> 2 cups finely chopped onions
> 2 medium baking potatoes, peeled and chopped (2 cups)
> 7 cups chicken stock (page 84)
> 2$^1/_2$ cups fresh shelled peas (2$^1/_2$ pounds in shells)
> 2 teaspoons salt
> $^1/_2$ teaspoon freshly ground black pepper
> 2 teaspoons fresh lemon juice

In a large soup pot over medium heat, melt the butter. Add the olive oil and onions and sauté for 10 minutes, until the onions appear glossy. Make sure they do not brown. Add the potatoes and chicken stock and bring to a boil. Lower the heat, cover the pot, and simmer for 30 minutes. Add the peas, salt, and pepper. Cook uncovered for 2 minutes longer. Cool. Add the lemon juice and puree the soup in batches in a blender until smooth. Cover and chill in the refrigerator.

YIELDS 4 TO 6 SERVINGS

Fresh peas can be found
from early May
through July. Choose
bright green, shiny,
medium-size pods. You
can use frozen petit
pois during the rest of
the year. We find them
to be the next best
thing to fresh.

Peach, buttermilk, and yogurt soup

I remember this sweet and very special chilled soup from my childhood. Special because, since peaches didn't grow in the Schleswig Holstein area where we lived, my mother had to wait for those rare and costly shipments of fresh peaches that came from southern Germany, France, or Italy.

> *3 pounds ripe fresh peaches, peeled, pitted,*
> *and cut into chunks*
> *1 cup buttermilk*
> *³/₄ cup plain yogurt*
> *¹/₃ cup sugar*
> *¹/₄ cup heavy cream*
> *¹/₂ cup apple juice*
> *¹/₄ cup fresh lemon juice*
> *1 teaspoon ground ginger*
> *Mint leaves for garnish*

In a large bowl, combine all the ingredients except the mint. Using a blender, puree the mixture in batches. Chill for at least 3 hours. Serve in glass bowls garnished with the mint leaves.

YIELDS 6 SERVINGS

Chilled cucumber soup

Garnish this soup with thin cucumber slices, a bit of crème fraîche, and chopped tender chives. It is so refreshing.

2 tablespoons butter
3 cups chopped onions
1/3 cup flour
2 European cucumbers (see Note), halved, seeded, and cut
into 2-inch pieces
5 cups chicken stock (page 84)
2 teaspoons salt
1/2 teaspoon ground white pepper
1/2 cup heavy cream
Chopped chives, crème fraîche, thin slices of cucumber for garnish

In a large, heavy saucepan over very low heat, sauté the butter and onions for 10 minutes. Make sure the onions do not brown. Add the flour and stir to combine. Add the cucumbers, chicken stock, salt, and pepper and bring to a boil. Lower the heat and simmer, covered, for 20 minutes, stirring the soup a few times. Add the cream, remove from the heat, and let cool to room temperature.

In a blender, puree the soup in batches and chill it for at least 4 hours before serving. Garnish as you wish.

YIELDS 6 SERVINGS

NOTE: European or English cucumbers, long, with thin, unwaxed skins, are called "seedless," but they do have some seeds.

Main courses
for spring and summer

....

Spring and summer conjure up the most beautiful memories of outdoor dining at its best. The golden days tend to lift our spirits as we linger at a table with family and friends, enjoying a good bottle of wine and reveling in the splendor of the setting sun.

I hoped, from the very first day we opened the doors to our Inn, that some of our best and most memorable occasions would occur on our terrace. Happily, it has turned out to be so. We have had glorious parties for guests who reserved the entire Inn for a weekend to celebrate a special occasion. We have had wedding rehearsal dinners, with only the immediate families seated at beautifully set tables stretching the length of the terrace. We have had emotional gatherings when family members from all over the world were reunited for a landmark anniversary. Really heart-felt festive occasions when our roses were in full bloom, the trees verdant, and everywhere, inside and out, candlelight seemed to be dancing in time to the music.

The first order of business when planning any event is to decide on a main course, which should really be the star of the evening, and build the dinner around that. The biggest consideration is to try to create a perfect harmony of tastes, textures, and colors with the freshet fish, meat, or poultry available. Having such beautiful produce so near at hand is an added luxury.

The atmosphere you create for outside parties is as important as for those held indoors. I make sure that no matter where we decide to have the party, there will be flowers everywhere. Lots of them. Large vases of sunflowers seem to bring smiles to everyone. Our long-stemmed roses, freshly cut from the garden, seem to encourage the romantic nature in people. I've watched men and women lean carefully into a large bouquet, sniff the roses, then lovingly cup a flower, just to relish it for a moment.

Candles are also essential, especially when the sun is setting. We use glass hur-

ricane globes that protect the flames from insidious breezes. Even though I prefer the linens to be more casual during the summer season, I choose colorful plaid tablecloths and vibrantly colored napkins.

Selecting the right wine is also paramount. Wine should be bought at least two days before uncorking, so it has time to settle. We use large bowls filled with ice to keep the white wine, champagne, and juices chilled. A friend of mine fills a small bathtub in her house with ice and stores all the necessary drinks, including water there. When the party is over, all she does is pull the plug to allow the melted ice to drain away.

Although everyone has his or her own taste when it comes to wines, in the spring and summer I think of clean, crisp, uncomplicated whites and soft reds. There are obvious differences in the nuances of flavor and the textures of wines, and since we are called upon to make suggestions, we have come to know many of these fine points. Therefore, I have included wine suggestions to go with each main course recipe. They are based on what I like to drink and serve with each individual meal.

We've winnowed some of the very best recipes from our rather large selection. They are chosen for their diverse tastes, textures, and unique qualities. Then—because we tend to feed larger numbers than you may be likely to—we've streamlined the ingredients so as to make the recipes more accessible for smaller dinner parties.

Bon appétit!

> *The west yet glimmers with some streaks of day:*
> *Now spurs the lated traveler apace*
> *To gain the timely Inn.*

WILLIAM SHAKESPEARE

Seared tuna with wasabi cream

Since the fish is served very rare, it is essential that you use only the freshest tuna available. The spicy wasabi cream is a great accompaniment to this tender, meaty fish.

> $^1/_4$ cup strong brewed tea
> $^1/_4$ cup soy sauce
> $^1/_4$ cup dry sherry
> 1 teaspoon freshly ground black pepper
> $1^1/_2$ tablespoons peanut oil
> Four 8-ounce tuna steaks, $1^1/_2$ inches thick, trimmed of all
>   skin and dark meat
> $1^1/_2$ tablespoons wasabi
> 2 tablespoons water
> $^3/_4$ cup mayonnaise
> Small bunch chives, chopped, for garnish

With a fork, whisk together in a bowl, the tea, soy sauce, sherry, and pepper. Set aside.

In a large noncorrosive sauté pan, heat the peanut oil until it smokes. Using tongs for safety, place the tuna steaks in the pan. Over high heat, sauté the steaks 2 minutes on each side. Remove from the heat and add the liquid mixture, moving and turning the tuna steaks a few times so they are well coated. Return the pan to the heat and cook for 1 minute longer. Transfer the tuna steaks, which should be rare in the center, to 4 warm dinner plates.

In a bowl, stir the wasabi and water together until smooth. Fold in the mayonnaise. Distribute the wasabi cream among the 4 plates, then add a dollop to the top of each steak. Garnish with the chopped chives.

YIELDS 4 SERVINGS

THE WASABI CREAM IS EASY
TO ASSEMBLE AND CAN BE
MADE A DAY AHEAD,
COVERED AND
REFRIGERATED UNTIL
NEEDED.

WINE SUGGESTION

A LONG ISLAND OR
CALIFORNIA ROSÉ
WOULD BE EXCELLENT
WITH THIS DISH.

Striped bass with lemon-dill sauce

The mild, creamy herb sauce allows you to savor the wholesome taste of this delicate, meaty fish. It is equally wonderful with other lean white fish, such as red snapper. And it's great, trickled over cold seafood salads.

One 3-pound striped bass, filleted
2 teaspoons minced garlic
1 teaspoon coarse kosher salt
2 tablespoons softened butter
1 tablespoon fresh lemon juice
1 bunch watercress for garnish
Lemon slices for garnish

LEMON-DILL SAUCE

$1/4$ cup chopped fresh dill
$1/2$ teaspoon grated lemon peel
1 tablespoon fresh lemon juice
$1/4$ cup heavy cream
$1/4$ cup bottled clam juice
$1/8$ teaspoon cayenne
8 tablespoons (1 stick) hot melted butter

Preheat the broiler for 10 minutes.

Place the bass fillet, skin side down, on a large sheet pan. Mash the garlic, salt, butter, and lemon juice into a paste and rub it all over and into the bass fillet. Broil the fish 4 inches from the heat source for about 15 minutes, until the fish has browned and is cooked through. Remove from the broiler and transfer to a warm platter. Garnish with the watercress and lemon slices.

For the sauce, in a blender, blend together all the ingredients except the hot butter for 5 seconds. With the blender still running, add the hot butter in a slow, steady stream. Transfer to a warm sauceboat and serve with the striped bass.

YIELDS 6 SERVINGS AND 1 CUP OF SAUCE

THE LEMON-DILL SAUCE CAN BE MADE UP TO 5 DAYS AHEAD, AND STORED, COVERED AND REFRIGERATED. SERVE IT CHILLED OR, IF YOU PREFER A WARM SAUCE, REHEAT IN A SMALL PAN OVER LOW HEAT, UNTIL JUST WARM. DON'T LET THE SAUCE COME TO A BOIL.

WINE SUGGESTIONS

A WHITE BURGUNDY OR A LONG ISLAND CHARDONNAY ARE NATURALS WITH OUR STRIPED BASS FROM LONG ISLAND WATERS.

Lobster cakes

These are sublime seafood cakes that we like to present on a bed of Schnusch (page 130) with tarragon-chive sauce served on the side.

> 3 tablespoons olive oil
> $^1/_2$ cup coarsely chopped shallots
> $^1/_2$ cup coarsely chopped celery
> 1 garlic clove, minced
> $1^1/_2$ pounds cooked lobster meat
> $^3/_4$ cup mayonnaise
> $^1/_2$ cup Homemade Bread Crumbs (see page 108)
> 1 teaspoon Dijon mustard
> 1 tablespoon capers with their brine
> $^3/_4$ teaspoon salt
> 1 tablespoon finely chopped fresh parsley
> 1 tablespoon finely chopped fresh tarragon
> 1 tablespoon butter

In a skillet, heat 1 tablespoon of the olive oil and sauté the shallots and celery over low heat for about 10 minutes, stirring often. Add the garlic and sauté for 1 minute longer. Remove from the heat and scrape the mixture into a large mixing bowl.

Place the lobster meat in the bowl of your food processor and pulse 4 times, until coarsely chopped. Transfer to the mixing bowl. Add the rest of the ingredients except the butter and remaining olive oil. With your hands, mix until well blended. Shape into eight 1-inch-thick patties.

Heat the butter and remaining 2 tablespoons of olive oil in a large skillet and sauté the lobster patties over medium heat for 5 minutes on each side, until they're crispy, browned, and cooked through. Serve hot.

YIELDS 4 SERVINGS AS A MAIN DISH
AND 8 AS A FIRST COURSE

YOU CAN PREPARE AND
FORM THE CAKES A DAY
AHEAD AND KEEP THEM
COVERED AND STORED IN
THE REFRIGERATOR. WHEN
READY TO SAUTÉ, ADD
ANOTHER MINUTE OF
COOKING TIME TO ADJUST
FOR THE CHILLED PATTIES.

WINE SUGGESTIONS

TRY AN ALSACE
PINOT-GRIS OR A
CHABLIS PREMIER
CRU. BOTH WINES
HAVE A LEVEL OF
RICHNESS THAT
COMPLEMENTS THIS
DISH.

(continued)

HOMEMADE BREAD CRUMBS

THERE'S NOTHING THAT BEATS THE TASTE OF HOMEMADE BREAD CRUMBS. THIS IS AN EASY RECIPE THAT CAN BE PREPARED IN MINUTES. COVERED AND STORED IN A COOL PLACE, THE BREAD CRUMBS WILL KEEP FOR UP TO 2 WEEKS.

1 loaf French bread, cut into $\frac{1}{2}$-inch-thick slices

PREHEAT THE OVEN TO 300°F.

SET THE BREAD SLICES IN 1 LAYER ON A BAKING SHEET. PLACE IN THE OVEN AND DRY FOR 20 MINUTES. TRANSFER TO THE BOWL OF YOUR FOOD PROCESSOR AND, USING THE METAL BLADE, PROCESS THE BREAD TO FINE CRUMBS 3 TO 4 MINUTES.

YIELDS APPROXIMATELY 3 CUPS BREAD CRUMBS

Salmon baked in ginger sauce

The fresh salmon pinks up beautifully, and with this pungent, spicy sauce, it is an outstanding entrée.

1 tablespoon peanut oil

1½ pounds skinless and boneless salmon fillets

¼ cup finely chopped fresh gingerroot

Grated rind of 1 lime

Juice of 1 lime

1 garlic clove, minced

⅓ cup rice vinegar

⅓ cup soy sauce

2 tablespoons toasted sesame oil

3 tablespoons dark brown sugar

2 scallions, sliced, for garnish

Preheat the oven to 400°F.

Brush a sheet pan with the peanut oil. Cut the salmon into 4 equal parts and place them on the oiled sheet pan.

The remaining ingredients, except for the scallions, go into a blender. Puree for 10 seconds until smooth. Pour the sauce over the salmon and bake for 12 minutes. To test for doneness, insert a knife into the thickest part of the fillet. The flesh should be flaky. Spoon the pan juices over the salmon and serve hot or at room temperature.

YIELDS 4 SERVINGS

WINE SUGGESTIONS

EITHER A CHASSAGNE-MONTRACHET OR A
CALIFORNIA CHARDONNAY IS SUPERB
WITH THIS RICH DISH.

Broiled or grilled swordfish with tomato-basil relish

Quick and easy, with a savory relish that gives it a zesty lift. Leftovers can transform a simple salad into a gratifying meal.

> *Six 8-ounce swordfish steaks, cut $^3/_4$ inch thick*
> *$^1/_4$ cup olive oil*
> *2 tablespoons fresh lemon juice*
> *$1^1/_2$ teaspoons salt*
> *$1^1/_2$ teaspoons coarsely ground fresh pepper*

TOMATO-BASIL RELISH

> *3 ripe tomatoes (about 1 pound)*
> *2 garlic cloves, minced*
> *$^1/_2$ cup finely chopped red onion*
> *4 anchovy fillets, minced*
> *$^1/_4$ cup olive oil*
> *Juice of $^1/_2$ lemon*
> *2 tablespoons drained capers*
> *$^1/_4$ cup finely chopped black oil-cured olives*
> *$^1/_4$ teaspoon salt*
> *1 cup finely chopped fresh basil leaves plus whole fresh*
>   *basil leaves for garnish*
> *1 lemon, cut into wedges*

Place the swordfish steaks in a shallow casserole dish. In a bowl, combine the olive oil, lemon juice, salt, and pepper and brush the mixture over the steaks. Marinate for 30 minutes at room temperature. Preheat the broiler for 15 minutes. Transfer the swordfish to a broiler pan and broil for 5 to 7 minutes on each side.

For the relish, chop the tomatoes very fine. Combine with all the rest of the ingredients except for the whole basil leaves and lemon wedges.

Transfer the cooked steaks to a large serving platter or 6 individual plates. Garnish with the whole basil leaves and lemon wedges and offer the relish on the side.

YIELDS 6 SERVINGS

WINE SUGGESTION

DRY SAUVIGNON BLANC FROM CALIFORNIA IS PERFECT. THIS WINE SHOULD BE VERY COLD, SO KEEP IT ON ICE IF YOU'RE SERVING THE FISH OUT OF DOORS.

Bouillabaise with rouille

This rich, savory soup combines the freshest, most succulent seafood available during the summer season. And all from our local waters!

1/4 cup olive oil

2 leeks, white parts only, cut into rings

4 cups sliced onions

6 garlic cloves, peeled and crushed

4 large ripe tomatoes, chopped

2 teaspoons saffron

1/2 teaspoon red hot pepper flakes

1 teaspoon fennel seeds

2 bay leaves

3 sprigs fresh thyme

1 1/2 cups white wine

6 cups fish stock (page 83)

Two 1 1/2-pound lobsters

1 1/2 pounds bass or anglerfish fillets

3/4 pound sea scallops

1 pound raw shrimp, peeled

24 littleneck clams

12 slices French bread, toasted

6 tablespoons freshly grated Gruyère cheese

2 tablespoons finely chopped fresh flat-leaf parsley

THE ROUILLE

4 garlic cloves

1/2 cup homemade bread crumbs

1/4 teaspoon cayenne

1/4 teaspoon saffron

2 tablespoons hot water

3 egg yolks

1 cup olive oil

In a large saucepan, heat the oil and sauté the leeks and onions over medium heat for 10 minutes. Don't let the vegetables brown. Add the garlic, tomatoes, saffron, pepper flakes, fennel seeds, and bay leaves. Stir to blend. Add the thyme, wine, and fish stock.

As the stock simmers, cut the tails and claws from the lobsters and set them aside. Cut the lobster bodies in half crosswise. Rinse the pieces clean and add them to the stock mixture. Bring to a boil. Lower the heat, cover, and simmer for 35 to 40 minutes.

Strain the soup into another large saucepan, pressing hard on the solids to remove all the juices. Discard the solids. Cut the fish fillets into large chunks. Cut the lobster tails into 3 pieces each. Add both to the strained soup. Crack the lobster claws and add them to the soup. Then add the scallops, shrimp, and clams. Cover and bring to a boil. Lower the heat and simmer the soup for 15 minutes, or until all the fish is cooked through and the clams have opened.

To make the rouille, place the garlic, bread crumbs, cayenne, saffron, and hot water in the bowl of a food processor. Process to a smooth consistency. Add the egg yolks. With the motor running, add the olive oil, first in droplets, then, as it starts to thicken, in a steady stream.

To serve the bouillabaisse, place 2 toasted bread slices in each of 6 heated soup plates. Dab each slice with rouille and some Gruyère cheese. Divide the fish and shellfish among the 6 plates. Ladle the broth over the fish. Sprinkle each serving with chopped parsley. The remaining rouille can be passed around the table.

YIELDS 6 SERVINGS

WINE SUGGESTIONS

A RIESLING FROM ALSACE OR A PINOT BLANC, ARE LIGHT, CRISP, AND COOL CHOICES TO COMPLEMENT THE FISH STEW.

Grilled cornish hens with lemon-orange sauce

You can prepare the hens the night before and leave them to marinate in the refrigerator until you're ready to grill them outdoors or broil them inside. If boneless chicken breasts are your preference, allow 1 half-breast per person. The sweet and pungent sauce elevates a conventional chicken dish into an exquisitely elegant meal.

4 small Cornish hens, $^3/_4$ to 1 pound each
6 ounces frozen orange juice concentrate
$^1/_2$ cup fresh lemon juice
$^2/_3$ cup honey
3 tablespoons tomato paste
3 garlic cloves, minced
Grated rind of 1 orange
Grated rind of 1 lemon
1 teaspoon fresh thyme leaves
1 teaspoon salt
$^1/_4$ teaspoon cayenne
Fresh thyme sprigs, for garnish

Split the hens in half. Remove the backbone and wing tips and save in your freezer for making stock.

Set the hens, cut side down, in a large shallow dish.

In a food processor, puree all the remaining ingredients except the thyme sprigs until they're smooth. Pour the mixture over the hens, cover, and marinate in the refrigerator for at least 4 hours or overnight.

One hour before serving time, remove the hens from the refrigerator. Preheat the grill (or the broiler). When the coals are almost white, place the hens, skin side down, on the grill (or in a broiler pan) approximately 3 inches from the heat. Grill (or broil) for 10 minutes, or until the hens are brown. Turn the hens and grill for 10 minutes on the other side.

Pour the marinade into a small saucepan and bring to a full rolling boil. Remove from the heat.

To serve, place 2 hen halves on each of 4 plates. Pour a little sauce over and around the hens. Garnish with the thyme sprigs and serve hot.

YIELDS 4 SERVINGS

WINE SUGGESTIONS

BEST WITH A COOL
BEAUJOLAIS OR A
ST.-VÉRAN; RED OR
WHITE IS A MATTER OF
PERSONAL TASTE.
I PREFER THE WHITE.

Parsley-crusted roast beef tenderloin with mustard sauce

The tenderloin can be served hot but is equally delicious served at room temperature. This is a very simple recipe that can be prepared up to 24 hours before serving time. Simply roast the tenderloin, then cover and refrigerate it. When ready to serve, cut the tenderloin into 1/2-inch slices and serve with the mustard sauce on the side. Leftovers, as you can imagine, make the best sandwiches.

One 5-to-6-pound beef tenderloin, trimmed of all fat
1 tablespoon salt
2 teaspoons freshly ground black pepper
2 cups finely minced fresh curly parsley
Grated rind of 1 lemon
1 garlic clove, very finely minced

THE MUSTARD SAUCE

1/2 cup Dijon mustard
2 tablespoons honey mustard
1 tablespoon drained, crushed, and minced green peppercorns

Preheat the oven to 500°F.

Rub the salt and pepper all over the beef tenderloin and place the beef in a roasting pan. Roast, uncovered, for 20 minutes. The beef will be rare. Cover it with foil and let it rest in a warm place for 20 minutes.

Mix together the parsley, lemon rind, and garlic. Spread the mixture over a clean sheet pan. Roll the tenderloin over the parsley mixture, making sure it adheres to the meat.

To make the mustard sauce, combine all the ingredients in a small bowl. Stir well to blend and serve on the side.

YIELDS 6 SERVINGS
WITH LEFTOVERS FOR SANDWICHES

WINE SUGGESTIONS

TRY A ST.-EMILION
GRAND CRU FROM
BORDEAUX OR A RED
ZINFANDEL FROM
SONOMA.

Grilled leg of spring lamb

A delicate yet robust meat that becomes a wonderful centerpiece for a special dinner. At the Inn, we serve this with an assortment of roasted vegetables and a bowl of Rhubarb Compote (recipe follows) on the side.

One 5-to-6-pound leg of spring lamb, boned and butterflied

THE MARINADE

$^1/_2$ cup Dijon mustard
$^1/_2$ cup sherry vinegar
$^1/_2$ cup soy sauce
$^1/_2$ cup honey
3 garlic cloves, crushed
1 tablespoon finely chopped fresh ginger
$^1/_2$ cup olive oil
1 teaspoon freshly ground black pepper

Place the lamb in a large shallow dish.

Combine the marinade ingredients in a food processor and process until smooth. Pour the marinade over the lamb, cover, and refrigerate for 1 to 3 hours.

Remove 1 hour before grilling. Reserve the marinade. When the coals are white hot, grill the lamb for 8 to 10 minutes on each side, until the meat is just springy to the touch. (For broiling, see sidebar.)

Set the lamb aside to rest for 5 minutes, then slice it thin and place it on a warm platter. Heat the marinade over a low flame until hot and pour it over the lamb.

YIELDS 6 SERVINGS

THE BEST-TASTING MEAT IS FROM
LAMB THAT IS 5 MONTHS OLD. THE
COLOR SHOULD BE LIGHT RED OR
DARK PINK. IF THE LEG IS LARGER,
7 TO 8 POUNDS, IT WOULD BE FROM
A MORE MATURE LAMB, ALSO
EXCELLENT BUT WITH A FULLER
FLAVOR MORE SUITABLE FOR
WINTER DINNERS.

THE LAMB CAN BE BROILED
INSTEAD OF GRILLED. PREHEAT
THE BROILER, PLACE THE LAMB ON
A RACK, AND BROIL FOR ABOUT 8
MINUTES ON EACH SIDE.

Rhubarb compote

2¹/₂ pounds rhubarb, cut into 1-inch pieces
1¹/₂ cups sugar
¹/₃ cup water
15 fresh mint leaves, chopped (optional)

In a heavy saucepan, combine all the ingredients except the mint leaves. Cover and cook over very low heat, stirring a few times, for 30 minutes, or until the rhubarb is tender. Pour the compote into a bowl and chill overnight. Stir in the chopped mint leaves and serve cold or at room temperature.

YIELDS 6 SERVINGS

(continued)

For special occasions, serve a soft Nebbiolo wine from the Piedmont region of Italy. Or a red Zinfandel from California.

CURRIED APRICOT MAYONNAISE

THIS CAN BE SERVED AS A DIP WITH CUT-UP PINEAPPLES, MELONS, AND BANANAS. IT COULD ALSO BE USED AS A SANDWICH SPREAD WITH LEFTOVER SLICED LAMB.

3 cups mayonnaise
$^1/_2$ cup apricot jam
2 tablespoons curry powder

IN A BOWL, COMBINE THE INGREDIENTS UNTIL THEY'RE WELL BLENDED. STORE IN THE REFRIGERATOR AND USE AS NEEDED.

YIELDS 3$^1/_2$ CUPS

Grilled veal chops with peach and coriander relish

The sweetness of peaches and the pungency of coriander seem to enhance the subtle taste of veal. This is one of our most popular summer entrées.

2 tablespoons olive oil
Six 1¼-inch-thick veal chops, well trimmed, bone
    scraped clean
1 tablespoon coarsely ground black pepper
1 teaspoon salt

PEACH AND CORIANDER RELISH

5 large (6 small) ripe peaches, peeled, pitted, and
    finely chopped
½ cup finely chopped green bell pepper
½ cup finely chopped red bell pepper
¾ cup red onion sliced into paper-thin rings
½ cup finely chopped fresh coriander leaves
2 jalapeño peppers, seeds removed, minced
2 tablespoons fresh lime juice
2 tablespoons olive oil

Prepare the grill so that the coals are almost white before you start.

Rub each veal chop with the olive oil. Then rub each chop with ½ teaspoon of pepper. Salt the veal on both sides. Grill the chops for 7 to 8 minutes on each side. The chops are done if the juices run clear when the meat is pierced with a fork. Keep the veal chops warm in a 200°F. oven for up to 30 minutes, or until you are ready to serve.

(continued)

To make the relish, combine all the ingredients in a bowl and toss to blend. Serve the relish on the side of the plate.

YIELDS 6 SERVINGS

....

WINE SUGGESTIONS

WE OFFER A RED AND A WHITE WINE WITH THIS DISH SUCH AS A PETIT SYRAH FROM CALIFORNIA AND A POUILLY-FUISSÉ FROM FRANCE.

....

Blanquette of veal
with spring vegetables

The bouquet garni, a mixture of aromatic herbs, is what brings the blanquette sauce to life. A full and satisfying meal that we serve with Basmati Rice Pilaf.

6 tablespoons butter

4 cups finely chopped onions

3 pounds stewing veal, cut from the shoulder, cubed

$^1/_2$ cup flour

1 cup dry white wine

$3^1/_2$ cups chicken stock (page 84)

$1^1/_4$ cups finely chopped celery

1 bouquet garni

1 tablespoon kosher salt

2 teaspoons freshly ground black pepper

$1^1/_2$ cups baby carrots, peeled and left whole

12 spring onions, with about 3 inches of green left on

$^3/_4$ pound asparagus, cut into $1^1/_2$-inch pieces

$^1/_3$ pound fresh spinach leaves

2 tablespoons minced fresh parsley, for garnish

Preheat the oven to 375°F.

Using a large stovetop-to-oven saucepan, melt the butter and sauté the onions over medium heat for 5 minutes. Add the meat and, stirring a few times, let the mixture stew for 10 minutes. Do not let the veal brown. Add the flour and stir gently to combine. Add the wine, chicken stock, celery, bouquet garni, salt, and pepper. Stir gently. Bring the mixture to a boil. Remove from the heat, cover tightly, and bake for 1 hour. Add the baby carrots and spring onions and bake for another 30 minutes. Add the asparagus and spinach and bake for 15 minutes longer.

Sprinkle with parsley and serve hot.

YIELDS 6 SERVINGS

TO MAKE YOUR OWN FRESH
BOUQUET GARNI, COMBINE
SPRIGS OF THYME, PARSLEY,
AND A BAY LEAF, OR ANY
COMBINATION OF HERBS YOU
PREFER, AND TIE THEM IN A
BUNDLE WITH COTTON STRING
SO THEY CAN BE RETRIEVED
AFTER COOKING. YOU MIGHT
WANT TO USE A SMALL RIB OF
CELERY TO HOLD THEM MORE
FIRMLY IN PLACE.

WINE SUGGESTION
WE LIKE A SOFT RED
SUCH AS PINOT NOIR
FROM CALIFORNIA.

Fresh goat cheese gnocchi

These scrumptious little dumplings are exceptionally light and completely grati-fying as a main course or, in smaller quantities, as a first course. We serve them in a tomato sauce with a light sprinkling of freshly grated Prince de Claverolle cheese, which is aged and adds just the right amount of bite.

> *4 cups water*
> *2 tablespoons butter*
> *1 cup finely minced onions*
> *2 cups goat curd*
> *2 cups cottage cheese*
> *4 egg yolks*
> *1 cup flour*
> *1 teaspoon salt*

THE SAUCE

> *2 tablespoons olive oil*
> *1 cup finely chopped onions*
> *4 cups finely chopped peeled tomatoes*
> *4 garlic cloves, minced*
> *1 teaspoon salt*
> *$1/2$ teaspoon freshly ground black pepper*
> *1 tablespoon finely sliced fresh chives*

Pour the water (at least 4 inches), into a large saucepan and place over high heat.

In a skillet, melt the butter and sauté the onions over medium heat for 5 minutes, until they're transparent.

In a bowl, combine the goat curd, cottage cheese, and egg yolks. Stir well. Add the sautéed onions, flour, and salt. Mix to blend. Spoon the mixture into a large pastry bag with a ^{1}/$_2$-inch plain tip. Pipe 1-inch-long pieces into the simmering water. The gnocchi are done when they float up to the surface of the water. Remove them with a slotted spoon onto a plate lined with a clean kitchen towel.

To make the sauce, in a skillet, heat the olive oil and sauté the onions over medium heat for 5 minutes, or until they turn transparent. Add the tomatoes, garlic, salt, and pepper. Bring the mixture to a boil. Lower the heat and simmer for 10 minutes.

To serve, divide the sauce among 4 warm dinner plates. Place the gnocchi on top of the sauce. Sprinkle with chives and serve warm.

YIELDS 4 TO 6 SERVINGS

WINE SUGGESTION

A CRISP DRY
SANCERRE, WELL
CHILLED, IS THE
CHOICE HERE.

Side dishes
for spring and summer

Spring and summer are the seasons when fresh vegetables abound. You can find freshly picked sweet corn, beautiful vine-ripened tomatoes, and a wide variety of farm-grown greens at almost any one of the many vegetable stands dotting the countryside. All of these vegetables can be prepared in a myriad of ways. Slice up eggplants; zucchini; mushrooms; red, yellow, or green peppers; carrots—almost any vegetable—brush them with a little oil, and pop them onto the grill. Easy, delicious, and nutritious. Steam some greens, add butter, a squeeze of lemon, and you have a satisfying side dish. Or you can eat the greens raw. I always have a bowl of raw sugar snap peas on my table. People seem to love that. The bowl gets refilled several times a day, especially when my grandchildren drop by for a visit.

What I have devised here are a variety of side dish recipes that not only take *advantage of the abundance of fresh vegetables but are also unique and quite tasty. All can be served at room temperature, which makes them ideal for indoor or out-door parties. Some are simple and earthy yet add beauty, color, and taste to any meal.*

Oven-roasted potatoes with fresh rosemary

We use firm, freshly harvested golden potatoes for this simple, earthy recipe.

2$^{1}/_{2}$ to 3 pounds Yukon Gold potatoes, or other firm and golden potatoes
$^{1}/_{3}$ cup olive oil
1 tablespoon coarse kosher salt
1 tablespoon finely chopped fresh rosemary
1 garlic clove, mashed

Preheat the oven to 450°F.

Cut the potatoes into wedges or bite-size pieces and place them in a bowl. Add the remaining ingredients and mix to coat well. Spread the potatoes in a single layer on a large heavy sheet pan. Roast for 35 to 40 minutes, or until the potatoes are crusty brown and cooked through. Serve hot.

YIELDS 6 SERVINGS

Schnusch with tarragon-chive sauce

All the mothers, grandmothers, anyone I knew who fed a family, had their own version of this fricassee of spring vegetables. My mother added new potatoes and made her sauce with hot cream and fresh chives. With it she served Westphalián Schinken. Try this with Lobster Cakes (page 106) crowning the vegetables and trickled with this creamy sauce.

$^3/_4$ pound white asparagus, peeled and cut into
    2-inch pieces
$^1/_2$ pound very young green beans, trimmed
$^1/_2$ pound baby carrots, trimmed
1 cup shelled fresh peas (1 pound with shells)
1 tablespoon butter
$^3/_4$ teaspoon salt

TARRAGON-CHIVE SAUCE

$^3/_4$ cup cooked fresh peas
2 tablespoons fresh tarragon leaves
$^1/_4$ cup chopped fresh chives
$1^1/_4$ cups hot half and half
$^1/_2$ teaspoon salt
4 drops Tabasco sauce
1 tablespoon fresh lemon juice

1 tablespoon chopped fresh chives for garnish
4 sprigs tarragon, for garnish

Fill a pot with 4 inches of water and cook the asparagus for 20 to 25 minutes, until they're tender. Drain and set aside. Cook the green beans for 5 minutes. Drain and set aside. The carrots should be cooked for 10 to 12 minutes, until they're tender. Drain and set aside. Cook the fresh peas in 1 inch of water for 1 minute only. Drain and set aside.

To make the sauce, puree the cooked peas, tarragon leaves, and chives in a blender, for 5 seconds. Pour the hot half and half into the blender and add the salt, Tabasco, and lemon juice. Blend for 10 seconds, until the sauce is smooth. Spoon the sauce onto 4 warm dinner plates.

Melt the butter in a sauté pan. Add the vegetables, sprinkle with salt, and sauté over medium heat until they're just heated through. Divide the vegetable mixture among the 4 plates, placing them on top of the sauce. Garnish with chives and tarragon leaves.

YIELDS 4 SERVINGS

Wheatberries with arugula and dried berries

For this we use a variety of dried fruits, such as strawberries, blueberries, cherries, and raisins. It's a mix-and-match salad that is always a huge success, especially for picnics. It's best to prepare the wheatberries the night before.

1½ cups wheatberries
3 quarts cold water
1 European cucumber (see Note page 97), halved lengthwise, seeded,
    diced into ½-inch pieces
1 cup finely chopped celery
1 cup mixed dried fruits
⅓ cup red wine vinegar
½ cup olive oil
1 teaspoon mustard
1½ teaspoons salt
½ teaspoon freshly ground black pepper
2 bunches fresh arugula, stems removed

Place the wheatberries in a large saucepan. Add the water and bring to a boil. Remove from the heat, cover tightly, and let stand overnight.

When ready to finish the salad, drain the wheatberries. You will find that most of the water will have been soaked up. Place the wheatberries in a large bowl. Add the cucumber, celery, and dried fruits.

In a jar, combine the vinegar, oil, mustard, salt, and pepper. Shake to blend. Pour over the wheatberries and toss well. Add the arugula and toss lightly.

YIELDS 4 TO 6 SERVINGS

Corn and tomato with cilantro

A colorful and marvelous addition to any buffet, this wholesome salad exemplifies summer vegetables at their best.

>   8 ears fresh corn, husked
>   3 medium tomatoes (about 1½ pounds)
>   2 teaspoons red wine vinegar
>   3 tablespoons full-bodied, virgin olive oil
>   ¾ teaspoon salt
>   ½ teaspoon freshly ground black pepper
>   ½ cup finely chopped fresh cilantro

Bring a large pot of water to a rapid boil. Plunge the ears of corn into the pot and cook for 5 minutes. Using tongs, remove the corn and set it on a platter to cool.

Using a knife in a downward motion, cut the kernels from the cobs and place the kernels in a bowl. Chop 1 tomato into bite-size pieces and add it to the corn. Add the vinegar, olive oil, salt, pepper, and cilantro and toss lightly to mix. Thinly slice the remaining 2 tomatoes and arrange the slices around the rim of a deep plate. Spoon the corn and tomato mixture into the center and serve at room temperature.

YIELDS 6 SERVINGS

DO NOT SALT THE CORN
DURING COOKING. IT WILL
TOUGHEN THE KERNELS.

White beans with red onion and fresh mint leaves

³/₄ pound Great Northern dry white beans
5 cups water
1 medium onion, peeled and cut into quarters
2 garlic cloves
1 cup thinly sliced red onion rings
1 cup finely chopped celery
¹/₂ cup olive oil
¹/₃ cup red wine vinegar
1 teaspoon salt
¹/₂ teaspoon freshly ground black pepper
2 cups fresh mint leaves, loosely packed

In a bowl, cover the beans with cold water and soak overnight. Drain and place the beans in a large saucepan. Add the water, quartered onion, and the garlic cloves. Bring to a boil, lower the heat, cover, and simmer for 1 to 1¹/₂ hours, until the beans are tender. The cooking time will depend on the age of the beans. Older beans need a longer cooking time. Drain the beans, discarding the onion and garlic. Set the beans aside to cool to room temperature.

Add the red onion rings, celery, olive oil, vinegar, salt, and pepper. Stir to mix well. Cut the mint leaves medium fine and add them to the beans just before serving.

YIELDS 4 TO 6 SERVINGS

You can prepare this the day before. Cover and refrigerate. One hour before serving time, remove from the refrigerator and taste. You may want to add a dash more vinegar and salt.

Peas, beans, and radish sprouts

Radish sprouts, with their deliciously peppery taste, add a special crispness to almost any salad or vegetable dish.

2 cups shelled young lima beans
2 cups shelled fresh peas
1 small basket radish sprouts
$^1/_4$ cup olive oil
2 tablespoons white wine vinegar
$^1/_2$ teaspoon Dijon mustard
1 garlic clove, crushed
1 teaspoon salt
$^1/_2$ teaspoon freshly ground black pepper

Place the lima beans in a saucepan, cover with water, and cook for 5 to 10 minutes, until they're done to your liking. Add the peas and cook for 1 minute longer. Drain, and pour the beans and peas into a bowl.

Trim the radish sprouts so that you are left with the tops and a 2-inch stem. Add the sprouts to the peas and beans.

In a separate bowl, whisk together all the remaining ingredients. Pour the dressing over the legumes and toss to blend. Serve hot, or chill the vegetables and serve them cold.

YIELDS 4 TO 6 SERVINGS

THE LIMA BEANS SHOULD
BE CHECKED AFTER
5 MINUTES OF COOKING.
THEIR DONENESS DEPENDS
ON THE AGE OF THE BEANS.
REMEMBER, THE OLDER
THEY ARE, THE LONGER
THE COOKING TIME.

White asparagus
with creamy lemon-herb sauce

An excellent first course. We serve this delicacy as a side dish with grilled meat or chicken. The sauce is just great over roasted meats, too.

> 2 pounds white asparagus
> 1 tablespoon finely chopped fresh parsley
> $^1/_2$ tablespoon chopped fresh tarragon
> 2 tablespoons fresh lemon juice
> $^1/_2$ teaspoon salt
> 2 egg yolks
> 8 tablespoons (1 stick) hot melted butter

Cut 1 inch off the bottom of each asparagus spear, then peel with a vegetable peeler, starting from the tip and going toward the base. Place the spears in a shallow saucepan and cover them with water. Bring to a boil. Lower the heat, cover, and simmer for 20 to 25 minutes, or until they're tender.

In a blender, puree the parsley, tarragon, lemon juice, and salt to a fine consistency. Add the egg yolks, blend, and, with the blender still running, add the hot butter in a slow, steady stream until the sauce is thickened and creamy.

Drain the asparagus and distribute them on 4 warm dinner plates. Spoon the lemon-herb sauce over the vegetables and serve.

YIELDS 4 SERVINGS

WHITE ASPARAGUS HAVE
FOR YEARS BEEN A
MUCH-PRIZED SPRING
DELICACY IN EUROPE. NOW
YOU CAN FIND THEM IN
MARKETS FROM EARLY MAY
TO LATE JUNE. THEY HAVE
ALWAYS BEEN ONE OF
MY FAVORITES.

Sauté of fresh spinach with garlic and pine nuts

3 tablespoons olive oil
1 garlic clove, minced
$^1/_4$ cup pine nuts
2 large bunches flat-leaf spinach, washed, dried, stems
    removed
$^1/_2$ teaspoon salt
$^1/_2$ teaspoon freshly ground black pepper

In a large stainless-steel sauté pan, heat the olive oil, garlic, and pine nuts over low heat. When the garlic and pine nuts start to sizzle, add the spinach all at once. Turn the heat to high and sauté for 4 to 5 minutes, stirring a few times until the spinach has wilted. Sprinkle with salt and pepper and serve hot.

YIELDS 4 SERVINGS

TO VARY THIS DISH, TRY
ADDING A HANDFUL OF
RAISINS AFTER THE PINE
NUTS. FOR A NUTTIER FLAVOR,
ADD 2 TABLESPOONS SESAME
SEEDS AND 1 TEASPOON
TOASTED SESAME OIL AND
PROCEED WITH THE RECIPE AS
WRITTEN.

Lemon rice with pine nuts

This easy-to-prepare side dish is best made 2 to 3 hours before serving. It goes beautifully with almost all fish and chicken dishes.

1 cup basmati rice, rinsed
$2^{1}/_{4}$ cups water
1 teaspoon salt
$^{3}/_{4}$ cup finely chopped celery
$^{1}/_{2}$ cup finely chopped scallions
Grated rind of $^{1}/_{2}$ lemon
$^{1}/_{3}$ cup toasted pine nuts

THE DRESSING

3 tablespoons fresh lemon juice
$^{1}/_{4}$ cup olive oil
$^{1}/_{2}$ teaspoon sugar
$^{1}/_{2}$ teaspoon salt

Place the rice in a saucepan, add the water and salt and bring to a boil. Stir once, then cover and simmer for 15 minutes. Transfer the rice to a bowl and let it cool to room temperature. Stir in the celery, scallions, lemon rind, and pine nuts.

Place all the dressing ingredients in a container with a tight-fitting lid and shake well. Pour the dressing over the rice and toss to blend well. Let the rice stand for a few hours to develop the flavors. Just before serving, taste and add more salt and lemon juice if needed.

YIELDS 4 SERVINGS

Sweet potato with fresh mint

This dish may seem oddly out of place in the "Spring-Summer" section, since sweet potatoes are customarily associated with fall and winter meals. However, at the end of July, when the new sweet potatoes appear in the markets, we scoop them up and turn them into this delectable side dish.

> 3 pounds new young sweet potatoes
> 1 bunch scallions
> 1 bunch fresh mint, leaves only
> 3 tablespoons red wine vinegar
> $^1/_2$ cup olive oil
> 1 teaspoon mustard
> 1 garlic clove, minced
> 1$^1/_2$ teaspoons salt
> $^3/_4$ teaspoon freshly ground black pepper

Cut the sweet potatoes into quarters. Place in a saucepan, cover with water, and bring to a boil. Lower the heat, cover, and allow the potatoes to simmer for 15 to 20 minutes, until they're cooked through. Drain and set aside to cool.

Remove the skin and cut the potatoes into bite-size pieces. Place them in a bowl. Cut the scallions, white and green parts, into thin rings. Add them to the potatoes along with the mint leaves.

Combine the remaining ingredients in a container with a tight-fitting lid. Shake well. Pour the dressing over the potatoes. Toss gently and serve.

YIELDS 5 TO 6 SERVINGS

Cheese and salad
for after dinner

Salad refreshes without weakening
and comforts without irritating.

BRILLAT-SAVARIN

I love a simple green salad and a fabulous cheese to follow the main course.

We have access to so many tender, young, fragile leafy greens in the spring and summer. Sometimes they are labeled "mesclun," which means "a mixture," and that is precisely what one gets—a gorgeous melange of watercress; young arugula leaves; small, smooth spinach leaves; butterhead lettuce; green oakleaf; red oakleaf; chervil leaves; purple basil leaves; baby cos lettuce; fresh mint leaves; and lemon balm. Who could ask for anything better?

I use two tablespoons of red wine vinegar or the very best balsamic vinegar one can buy; six tablespoons of a fragrant, fine olive oil; a little salt and pepper.

Then I toss the salad very carefully. Never douse it with lemon. Even a hint of lemon juice will destroy the gentleness of the leaves. Any combination of the above-mentioned greens, although no more than three, simply dressed, served with a selection of gorgeous cheeses, is truly a wonderful way to finish off a meal. I have found that guests will have that extra glass of wine and remain at the table when they see the salad and cheese tray arrive. Sometimes that's when the best conversation takes place because host, hostess, and guests are satiated, relaxed, and taking a breather before dessert makes its seductive entrance.

I have compiled a list of cheeses, favorites that we sell at Loaves and Fishes and serve at the Inn. We select one and serve it on the same dish as the salad or offer a variety of three that are complementary in flavors and textures. Because goat cheeses are made from fresh milk and do not need to be aged, they can be enjoyed throughout the summer. Cabridoux *is a creamy fresh, mild goat cheese.* Camembert chevre *is a wonderful, soft, ripening goat cheese from Poitou.* Caprini logs *or* Fresco *are mild, fresh-tasting goat cheeses that have a pleasant tang.* Clochette *is a charmingly bell-shaped goat cheese.* Gorgonzola *is rich, savory, and pungent.* Stilton, *a crumbly blue cheese from England, is also known as the King of Blue Cheese and believe me, when it's good, nothing beats it.* Mont Briac *is a soft blue, spreadable brie.* Saint-Albray *is a soft buttery, mild, cow's milk cheese.* L'Edel de Cleron *is creamy, brie-like, and gently pungent, and, may I add, a major favorite with our customers at Loaves and Fishes.* Explorateur *is another, equally wonderful, triple cream that is more piquant.* Saint-Nectaire *is semi-soft with a mellow-tangy finish.* Ubriaco *is buttery, with a delicate wine taste; and* Royal Provence *is a combination of cow and goat milk cheese that is truly excellent.*

Cheeses served after a main course are especially successful with certain fruits. A large bunch of tiny champagne grapes, for instance, is a guaranteed favorite. Also, fresh, juicy peaches; ripe apricots; or sweet and tangy plums all might have been created solely to be savored with any or all of these cheeses.

Cheese—milk's leap toward immortality.

CLIFTON FADIMAN

Desserts
for spring and summer

· ·

What wondrous life is this I lead!
Ripe apples drop about my head;
The luscious clusters of the vine
Upon my mouth do crush their wine;
The nectarine, and curious peach,
Into my hands themselves do reach.

ANDREW MARVELL

Strawberries, raspberries, blueberries, blackberries, peaches, apricots, plums,

nectarines, cherries, long stalks of fresh rhubarb. On their own, raw or poached,

nestled inside a porcelain bowl and doused with cream, encased in a flaky dough

crust, or blanketed between sweet and airy layers of meringue; these are summer's

true rewards.

Desserts are very important. They should produce tantalizing aromas, they

147

need to look great, and finally, their taste should surpass your guests' expectations. They should be sweet, they should be crunchy, and they should infinitely satisfy all of our senses.

I love making desserts. I get so excited by them because they allow me to create what will become the grand finale to a wonderful evening.

Each of the following recipes is a favorite both at Loaves and Fishes and with our guests at the Inn. Peaches and chocolate! Chocolate Tartlets with Black Cherries. The perennial and very popular rich Key Lime Pie. Rhubarb-Blackberry Crisp! And Red Grits, which I suppose at first glance may surprise you. It is scrumptious. I whipped up a batch at Loaves and Fishes and had it sitting in a pretty bowl, waiting to be taken to the Inn where there was a party planned for later that day. One of our regular customers popped in, saw it on the counter, and

Sliced Smoked Salmon on Grain Bread

Baba Ghanouj on Endive Leaves

Radish and Fresh Goat Cheese Canapés

Cucumber, Egg, and Caviar

Bruschetta with Summer Tomatoes and Basil

Shrimp, Horseradish, and Arugula on Rye Toast

Summer Borscht
Caraway Breadsticks

Peach-Chocolate Tart

Cucumber Salad

Rye Bread

Corn and Tomato with Cilantro

Striped Bass with Lemon-Dill Sauce

said she desperately needed to bring a dessert to a dinner party she was off to. She took the Red Grits and some crème fraîche and off she went. She was back the next day with the bowl cleaned out and asking for another order for a party she was having that night.

Read each recipe through so that you will have a clear idea of what you need before beginning. Whenever possible, try to assemble most of your dessert the day before so that all you need to do at serving time is add the final flourishes. Most of the recipes are not complicated. And those that at first seem complicated are well worth the extra effort.

Desserts add an exclamation point to your dinner party. If your dinner hasn't gone as well as you had hoped and you follow it with a knock-out dessert, that is what your guests will remember.

Peach pie

There's a wonderful peach orchard I pass on my way to the Inn. I can't wait for the middle of August when the PICK YOUR OWN PEACHES sign appears. The first moment I can get away, I'm there, eating peaches, ripe and juicy, warmed by the sun, while I fill my baskets full. Then back to the Inn I go where the perfume of fresh peaches fills the kitchen as I set about concocting all sorts of peach desserts.

THE CRUST

2 cups flour
$^1/_2$ teaspoon salt
12 tablespoons ($1^1/_2$ sticks) cold butter, cut into small pieces
4 to 5 tablespoons cold water

THE FILLING

6 cups peeled, pitted, and sliced fresh, ripe peaches
3 tablespoons cornstarch
$^3/_4$ cup sugar
$^1/_4$ teaspoon almond extract
$^1/_4$ teaspoon grated nutmeg
Grated rind of 1 orange

THE EGG WASH TOPPING

1 egg yolk
1 tablespoon cream
3 tablespoons sugar

Preheat the oven to 375°F.

Place the flour and salt in the bowl of a food processor fitted with a metal blade, add the cold butter and pulse 5 times. With the motor running, add the water. Process until the dough starts to stick together. Turn the dough onto a floured work surface and shape it into a ball. Cover and chill for 30 minutes.

Divide the dough in half. Roll out one half to an 11-inch circle and fit it into a 9-inch pie plate.

Combine the filling ingredients in a bowl and spoon the filling into the unbaked pie shell.

Roll out the remaining dough to a 10-inch circle. Fit it over the peach filling. Crimp the pie edges together to seal. Cut 6 slits in an attractive pattern into the top crust. This will allow the steam to escape.

For the topping, in a bowl, beat together the egg yolks and cream. Brush the egg wash over the pie and sprinkle with the sugar. Bake for 50 minutes, or until the crust is brown and the filling is bubbling. Cool to room temperature.

YIELDS 6 GENEROUS SERVINGS

Peach-chocolate tart

Sweet, juicy peaches and rich chocolate! I love making this tart. It's an all-time favorite at Loaves and Fishes and with our guests at the Inn. Serve it with tea or a
glass of sherry or on its own with a scoop of ice cream or crème fraîche. Any way,
it's memorable.

THE FILLING

8 large ripe peaches (or 10 medium), halved and pitted
$^1/_2$ cup sugar
5 ounces fine quality semi-sweet chocolate, cut into small pieces
$^1/_3$ cup apricot preserves

THE CRUST

$^1/_2$ cup sliced almonds
2 tablespoons sugar
$1^1/_4$ cups flour
8 tablespoons (1 stick) cold butter, cut into $^1/_2$-inch pieces
1 egg yolk
2 tablespoons cold water

Preheat the oven to 350°F.

For the filling, place the peach halves, skin side down, in a glass baking
dish. Sprinkle them with the sugar and bake for 20 minutes. Remove from the
oven and set aside to cool.

Set the oven to 400°F.

To make the crust, process the almonds and sugar until fine. Add the
flour and butter. Pulse 4 times. Add the egg yolk and water and pulse 6 times,
or until the dough is crumbly. Transfer the dough to a working surface and
gather it into a ball. Cover and chill for 30 minutes.

Roll the dough into a 12-inch round and fit it into a 9-inch tart pan with a removable bottom. Lightly prick the shell with a fork. Bake for 20 minutes or until golden brown.

Remove from the oven and sprinkle the bottom of the tart shell with the chocolate pieces. Let stand for about 5 minutes, until the chocolate has melted. Using the back of a spoon, spread the chocolate evenly over the bottom of the shell. Cool completely.

Cut the peach halves in half again and arrange them, cut side up, in a circular pattern, over the chocolate. Melt the apricot preserves in a small saucepan and brush the preserves over the peaches. Serve the tart at room temperature.

YIELDS 6 TO 8 SERVINGS

THE TART CAN BE MADE UP TO
6 HOURS AHEAD OF SERVING
AND KEPT AT ROOM
TEMPERATURE.

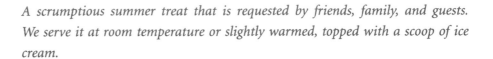

Rhubarb-blackberry crisp

A scrumptious summer treat that is requested by friends, family, and guests. We serve it at room temperature or slightly warmed, topped with a scoop of ice cream.

> 1 tablespoon cornstarch
> ¹/₄ cup water
> 1¹/₄ pounds fresh rhubarb, cut into 1-inch pieces
>   (5 cups)
> 1 cup granulated sugar
> ¹/₂ teaspoon ground cinnamon
> 2¹/₂ cups fresh blackberries

> THE TOPPING

> ¹/₂ cup flour
> ¹/₄ cup granulated sugar
> ¹/₂ cup light brown sugar
> ¹/₂ cup oatmeal
> ¹/₃ cup coarsely chopped walnuts
> ¹/₄ teaspoon ground cinnamon
> 4 tablespoons (¹/₂ stick) softened butter

Preheat the oven to 375°F.

In a heavy, small saucepan, stir the cornstarch and water together until they're smooth. Add the rhubarb and sugar. Cook over medium heat for about 10 minutes, stirring constantly, until the rhubarb is soft. Remove from the heat and fold in the cinnamon and blackberries. Blend well. Distribute the mixture into six 1-cup ramekins.

For the topping, in a bowl, combine all the ingredients. Mix well with your hands until crumbly. Sprinkle over the top of each ramekin. Place the ramekins on a baking sheet and bake for 25 minutes or until the crumbs are brown and beginning to bubble. Cool for 2 hours before serving.

YIELDS 6 SERVINGS

THE CRISP CAN BE MADE IN ONE 6-CUP RAMEKIN OR CASSEROLE DISH. SIMPLY INCREASE THE BAKING TIME TO 45 MINUTES.

Blueberry-rhubarb tart

Sweet and tangy. Delicious with Crème Anglaise (recipe follows), Crème fraîche, or vanilla ice cream. Or completely on its own.

THE CRUST

2¹/₂ cups flour
3 tablespoons sugar
12 tablespoons (1¹/₂ sticks) butter, cut into small pieces
2 egg yolks
5 tablespoons water

THE FILLING

5 or 6 stalks fresh rhubarb, cut into ¹/₂-inch pieces
    (5 cups)
1¹/₂ cups sugar
¹/₄ cup cornstarch
¹/₂ cup water
¹/₂ teaspoon ground cinnamon
Grated rind of 1 lemon
3 cups fresh blueberries

THE GLAZE

1 egg yolk
1 tablespoon heavy cream
3 tablespoons sugar

For the crust, place the flour, sugar, and butter in the bowl of a food processor. Pulse 5 times. Add the egg yolks and water and process until the dough starts to cling together. Gather the dough into a ball, cover it with waxed paper, and chill for 30 minutes.

Roll two-thirds of the dough into a 12-inch circle. Fit the circle into a 9-inch springform pan, pressing the dough onto the bottom and up the sides of the pan to form a 1-inch rim. Chill the prepared crust and the remaining pastry while working on the filling.

Preheat the oven to 375°F.

Using a heavy saucepan, cook the rhubarb and sugar over medium to high heat. Stirring often, bring the mixture to a boil. Immediately lower the heat, and simmer until the rhubarb releases its juices, which will happen very quickly. Remove from the heat and set aside.

Stir the cornstarch and water together in a bowl until it's smooth. Add to the rhubarb and stir continuously over a low heat until the mixture thickens. Fold in the cinnamon, lemon rind, and blueberries. Pour the filling into the chilled crust, spreading it evenly over the bottom.

Roll out the remaining pastry to $1/8$-inch thickness. Cut it into $1/2$-inch strips and create a lattice pie top by crisscrossing the strips over the tart filling.

For the glaze, in a bowl, beat together the egg yolk and cream. Lightly brush the mixture over the lattice strips. Sprinkle sugar over the tart top and bake for 1 hour, or until the fruit is bubbling and the crust appears light brown. Cool the tart for at least 2 hours.

Serve warm or cold.

YIELDS 7 TO 8 SERVINGS

(continued)

Crème anglaise

A wonderfully versatile custard sauce that can be poured over fresh fruits and cakes. It takes 10 minutes to make, excluding cooling time, and keeps up to 4 days in the refrigerator.

> *4 egg yolks*
> *$^1/_3$ cup sugar*
> *$1^3/_4$ cups milk*
> *1 teaspoon vanilla extract*

In a heavy saucepan, whisk the egg yolks and sugar until the mixture is light. Add the milk and whisk to blend. Set over medium heat and, stirring constantly with a wooden spoon, heat the custard until it starts to thicken. Don't allow it to boil or the eggs will curdle. Remove from the heat, add the vanilla, pour the custard into a glass pitcher, and let it cool.

YIELDS 2 CUPS

VANILLA BEANS IN VODKA

TO MAKE YOUR OWN VANILLA EXTRACT, PLACE 20 VANILLA BEANS IN A TALL, SLIM JAR. COVER WITH VODKA AND STORE AT ROOM TEMPERATURE FOR 3 WEEKS, UNTIL THE BEANS SOFTEN. TO USE, SNIP OFF THE END AND PRESS OUT AS MUCH VANILLA ESSENCE AS REQUIRED. RETURN THE USED BEANS TO THE JAR SINCE IT ALL HELPS TO TURN THE VODKA INTO VANILLA EXTRACT. THIS IS EXCELLENT FOR CRÈME ANGLAISE, PUDDINGS, AND PIE FILLINGS. WHEN A RECIPE CALLS FOR A TEASPOON OF VANILLA EXTRACT, USE THE VANILLA-FLAVORED VODKA.

Red grits with cream

My mother would serve this Scandinavian dessert following a large mid-day meal. At one time, it was thickened with barley meal or buckwheat, hence the name "grits." Once a humble regional specialty, grits is now served in crystal bowls at elegant dinner parties.

> *2 cups red currants or raspberries*
> *2 cups black currants or blackberries*
> *³/₄ cup sugar*
> *1 cup water*
> *¹/₄ cup potato starch or cornstarch*
> *1 tablespoon fresh lemon juice*
> *¹/₂ teaspoon ground cinnamon*
> *4 additional cups berries of your choice*
> *1 cup half and half*
> *¹/₂ cup heavy cream*

In a saucepan, combine the currants or berries, the sugar, and ³/₄ cup of the water. Stirring often, bring the mixture to a boil. Cook for 2 minutes.

In a small bowl, stir together the remaining ¹/₄ cup of water and the potato starch. Pour it into the berry mixture while it is still over the heat. Stir until the mixture thickens and becomes clear. Fold in the lemon juice, cinnamon, and the additional 4 cups of berries. Remove from heat and chill.

Serve chilled with half and half and heavy cream combined on the side.

YIELDS 6 SERVINGS

Summer berry pudding

＊

To get the full-bodied flavor of this dessert, it should be made 1 day ahead of the time you wish to serve it. We like to use the freshest and ripest berries and mix and match them: strawberries and blueberries or raspberries and blackberries.

THE WARM BERRY MIXTURE

2 cups raspberries
2 cups blueberries
1¼ cups sugar
½ cup water

THE FILLING

1 loaf homemade white bread or fine-grained
*   store-bought white*
2 cups raspberries
2 cups blueberries
2 cups sliced strawberries
2 fresh mint sprigs
1½ cups crème fraîche

To make the warm berry mixture, in a saucepan, combine all the ingredients. Place the pan over medium heat for about 10 to 12 minutes, and, stirring a few times, heat the mixture until the berries release some of their juices and the sugar has melted. Remove from the heat.

Line an 8-inch springform pan with a large piece of plastic wrap so that it overhangs the edges and you have enough to cover the pudding when you are finished.

For the filling, spoon some of the warm berry mixture over the bottom of the pan. Cut the bread into slices, then triangles. Fit the pieces snugly over the berry mixture. Spoon more berry mixture over the bread. Sprinkle with raw berries and continue layering with bread triangles, warm berry mixture, and raw berries until you have 3 layers of each, ending with a topping of raw berries. Save a cup of raw berries for garnishing the pudding.

Fold the overhanging plastic wrap over the pudding. Place a 7-inch plate on top of the plastic wrap, and weigh it with a large heavy can. Refrigerate for at least 12 hours or up to 48 hours.

When ready to serve, remove the plastic wrap from the top. Invert the pudding onto a serving plate. Remove the springform pan and plastic wrap. Garnish the pudding with the remaining berries and the mint sprigs.

To serve, cut the pudding into wedges as you would a cake. Offer the crème fraîche on the side.

YIELDS 6 TO 8 SERVINGS

Plum tart

We've added a delicious chewy layer made of rolled oats, nuts, and brown sugar to the bottom of this tart. It complements the tartness of the small Italian plums and adds a surprising texture and taste. We serve it slightly warmed with crème fraîche or Crème Anglaise (page 158) on the side.

THE CRUST

1¹/₂ *cups flour*
¹/₂ *teaspoon baking powder*
2 *teaspoons granulated sugar*
¹/₄ *teaspoon salt*
8 *tablespoons (1 stick) cold butter, diced into cubes*
1 *egg yolk*
1 *tablespoon fresh lemon juice*
3 *tablespoons water*

THE CRUMB LAYER

¹/₂ *cup flour*
¹/₂ *cup rolled oats*
¹/₂ *cup light brown sugar*
¹/₄ *cup granulated sugar*
¹/₄ *cup chopped walnuts*
¹/₄ *teaspoon ground cinnamon*
8 *tablespoons (1 stick) softened butter*

THE FILLING

2¹/₄ *pounds Italian plums*
2 *tablespoons butter*
¹/₃ *cup granulated sugar*

For the crust, place the flour, baking powder, sugar, and salt into the bowl of a food processor fitted with a metal blade. Pulse twice. Add the butter and pulse 5 times. Add the egg yolk and, with the motor running, add the lemon juice and water. Process until the pastry starts to stick together. Turn the dough onto a lightly floured work surface and knead it into a ball. Cover and chill for 30 minutes.

Meanwhile, preheat the oven to 375°F.

Place all the crumb layer ingredients into the food processor bowl. Pulse 3 times, until the mixture is crumbly.

For the filling, halve and pit the plums.

Roll the pastry into a 12-inch round and fit it into a 9-inch tart pan with a 1-inch rim. Prick the bottom with a fork. Bake the tart for 8 minutes. Remove and cool for 15 minutes.

Sprinkle the crumb mixture over the bottom of the pastry shell. Arrange the plums, cut side up, in a circular pattern over the crumb layer. Dot with the butter and sprinkle with the sugar. Bake for 45 to 50 minutes, or until the plums are soft and the edges have browned.

YIELDS 6 TO 8 SERVINGS

Strawberry meringue torte

Light and sweet, with a melt-in-your-mouth crunchiness, this was a traditional summer dessert in the Flensburg area where I grew up. Whatever fruit ripened in our garden was used between the layers of this cake. My mother always had lots of sweetened whipped cream to go along with the torte. Try this with any assortment of berries or with peaches. It is really a treat with a capital T.

8 tablespoons (1 stick) softened butter
$1\frac{1}{2}$ cups sugar
4 eggs, separated
1 cup cake flour
$1\frac{1}{2}$ teaspoons baking powder
2 tablespoons milk
2 teaspoons vanilla extract
1 cup sliced almonds

The filling

$1\frac{1}{4}$ cups heavy cream
2 tablespoons confectioners' sugar
Seeds of $\frac{1}{4}$ vanilla bean
1 pint strawberries, hulled

Preheat the oven to 350°F.

In a bowl, cream the butter and $\frac{1}{2}$ cup of the sugar with an electric mixer for about 5 minutes, until light in color. Add the 4 egg yolks and blend well. Add the cake flour, baking powder, milk, and 1 teaspoon of the vanilla and mix at low speed until well combined. Divide the batter between two 9-inch springform pans, spreading it evenly over the bottom of each pan. There will be just enough batter to cover them both.

In a clean mixing bowl, beat the egg whites until they hold soft peaks. With the mixer running on low, add the remaining cup of sugar. Then add 1 teaspoon of the vanilla extract. Spread half the meringue mixture on each unbaked cake layer. Sprinkle with the almonds, dividing them equally between the 2 pans. Bake for 25 to 35 minutes, until the tortes are evenly browned. Remove from the oven and cool.

For the fillings, in a bowl, beat the heavy cream, confectioners' sugar, and vanilla bean seeds until the cream holds soft peaks.

Invert 1 cake layer, meringue side down, on a flat cake plate. Spread it evenly with the whipped cream and top it with as many strawberries as possible. Place the second layer, meringue side up, on top of the strawberries. Surround the cake with any leftover strawberries.

YIELDS 8 TO 12 SERVINGS,
DEPENDING ON THE APPETITES OF YOUR FAMILY OR GUESTS.

Key lime pie

This rich, cool, tangy pie sells briskly throughout the summer months at Loaves and Fishes and is often requested by our guests at the Inn.

> *2 cups graham cracker crumbs*
> *¹/₂ cup plus 2 tablespoons sugar*
> *¹/₄ teaspoon ground cinnamon*
> *6 tablespoons melted butter*
> *6 egg yolks*
> *2 tablespoons evaporated milk*
> *1³/₈ cups sweetened condensed milk*
> *2 teaspoons grated lime rind*
> *¹/₂ cup fresh lime juice*
> *³/₄ cup heavy cream*
> *Seeds of ¹/₄ vanilla bean*
> *1 lime, cut into wedges*

Preheat the oven to 350°F.

Place the cracker crumbs, ¹/₂ cup sugar, the cinnamon, and butter in a bowl. Toss to blend slightly. Press the mixture onto the bottom and up the sides of a 9-inch pie plate. Bake for 8 minutes or until lightly browned. Remove from the oven and cool.

Using an electric mixer, beat the egg yolks until they're creamy. Add the evaporated and condensed milks and beat just to blend. Add the lime rind and juice, which will thicken the mixture. Mix to blend well. Pour the filling into the cooled graham cracker crust and smooth the top.

In a bowl, beat the heavy cream, 2 tablespoons sugar, and the vanilla seeds until the cream holds soft peaks. Spoon the whipped cream into a pastry bag fitted with a decorative tip. Pipe the cream onto the pie in a pattern of your choice.

Freeze the pie for at least 4 hours, then cover with plastic wrap if you want to freeze it longer. It will keep for up to 2 weeks when frozen. To serve, remove the pie from the freezer and wait for 20 minutes before serving. Garnish with the lime wedges.

YIELDS 6 SERVINGS

Chocolate-almond cake

A rich chocolate cake that, trickled with a delicious raspberry sauce and sprinkled with fresh raspberries, is superb.

THE CAKE

5 ounces unsweetened chocolate
8 tablespoons (1 stick) softened butter
1¼ cups sugar
6 eggs, separated
1 teaspoon vanilla extract
½ teaspoon almond extract
½ cup almonds
¼ cup flour
1 teaspoon baking powder

THE GLAZE

2 ounces semi-sweet chocolate
6 tablespoons softened butter
2 tablespoons strong brewed coffee

THE RASPBERRY SAUCE

2 pints fresh raspberries
½ cup sugar
1 tablespoon framboise (optional)
¼ cup water

Preheat the oven to 325°F. Butter a 9-inch springform pan.

For the cake, chop the chocolate into small pieces and place it in an oven-proof bowl. Inside the oven, melt the chocolate for about 5 minutes, or until it's soft. Set aside.

In a bowl, cream the butter and sugar together until they're light in color. Add the egg yolks, one at a time, beating after each addition. Stir in the vanilla and almond extracts.

In a food processor, combine the almonds, flour, and baking powder. Process until very fine. Add to the egg yolk mixture. Add the melted chocolate and beat at low speed until the batter has a smooth consistency. Spoon the mixture into a large mixing bowl.

Place the egg whites in the clean bowl of an electric mixer and, with clean beaters, beat until soft peaks hold. Fold in the chocolate batter in a careful rotating motion until all traces of the egg whites have disappeared. Spoon the batter into the prepared springform pan. Bake in the middle of the oven for 35 to 40 minutes, or until a toothpick inserted in the center of the cake comes out with a few crumbs attached. Do not overbake. Remove the cake from the oven and cool to room temperature. Transfer to a serving plate. You can do this the day before and store the cake, covered in plastic wrap, until ready to serve.

To make the glaze, preheat the oven to 325°F. Place the chocolate in an ovenproof bowl and melt it in the oven for 5 minutes. Stir in the butter and coffee. Using a spatula, spread the glaze over the top and sides of the cooled cake. Store the cake at room temperature until ready to serve.

For the raspberry sauce, place 1 pint of the raspberries in a food processor and add the sugar; framboise, if desired; and water. Process until smooth. Serve the cake in wedges drizzled with the raspberry sauce, and for the finishing touch, sprinkle the top with fresh raspberries.

If you have fresh mint in the garden, garnish each plate with a sprig.

YIELDS 1 CAKE, OR 8 TO 10 SERVINGS

Chocolate tartlets with black cherries and espresso crème anglaise

Gorgeous and scrumptious! A real treat with a cup of strong coffee midafternoon, or an ideal dessert following a light meal. The chocolate shells can be prepared a day ahead and stored at room temperature.

> *1 cup flour*
> *¼ cup unsweetened cocoa powder*
> *1 teaspoon instant espresso powder*
> *4 tablespoons (½ stick) butter*
> *6 tablespoons cream cheese*
> *¼ cup sugar*
> *1 egg yolk*
> *¾ cup semi-sweet chocolate chips*
> *1 pint black cherries, pitted*
> *¼ cup sugar*
> *1 tablespoon kirsch*
> *Espresso Crème Anglaise (recipe follows)*

Place the flour, cocoa, and espresso powder in the bowl of a food processor. Cut the butter and cream cheese into pea-size morsels and add them to the bowl. Add the sugar and egg yolk. Pulse until the dough starts to stick together. Remove it from the bowl, wrap it in plastic, and place it in the refrigerator to chill for 30 minutes.

Preheat the oven to 375°F. Butter twelve 2½-inch tartlet pans with removable bottoms. With your fingers, divide the dough into 12 equal pieces and press them into the tart pans, making sure to cover the bottom and sides of each pan. Bake for 10 minutes. Remove from the oven and distribute the chocolate chips evenly among the tartlet shells. Bake for 3 minutes to melt the chocolate. Cool.

In a bowl, combine the cherries, sugar, and kirsch and, just before serving, spoon some of the mixture on top of each chocolate shell. The espresso crème anglaise should be served on the side.

YIELDS 12 TARTLETS

Espresso crème anglaise

A versatile dessert sauce that can be used with sweet loaves, rich chocolate tarts, or simple puddings. At the Inn, we trickle this crème over fresh summer berries. It is absolutely delicious.

> *5 egg yolks*
> *1/2 cup sugar*
> *1 3/4 cups milk*
> *1/3 cup extra-strong brewed espresso*
> *1/2 teaspoon vanilla extract*

In a medium-size heavy saucepan, combine the egg yolks and sugar. Using a whisk, beat until they're creamy. Add the milk and espresso. Set the pan over medium heat and, stirring constantly, bring the mixture almost to a boil. Remove from the heat and keep stirring until the crème cools slightly. Stir in the vanilla and chill the sauce for 4 hours or more. When refrigerated, it will keep up to 4 days.

YIELDS 3 CUPS

Vanilla crème anglaise

Omit espresso from above recipe.

Wine-poached peaches served with crème fraîche

A delicate and pleasing finish to a big meal or a welcome surprise at breakfast. You can substitute fresh apricots if you prefer, by allowing 3 per person. This is a simple, foolproof recipe.

> 12 ripe yellow peaches
> $2^1/_2$ cups dry white wine
> $2^1/_2$ cups water
> $1^1/_2$ cups sugar
> 1 vanilla bean, split in half lengthwise
> 1 recipe Crème Fraîche (page 39)

Bring a saucepan half filled with water to a boil. Immerse the peaches in the water for 1 minute then remove them to a plate. When cool enough to handle, remove the skins. Discard the water.

In the same saucepan, combine the wine, water, sugar, and vanilla bean. Bring to a boil. Add the peeled peaches and simmer for 8 minutes, or until there is no resistance when the peaches are pierced with a toothpick. Remove the peaches with a slotted spoon. Continue cooking the liquid for 15 minutes longer over high heat to reduce it slightly. Pour the mixture over the peaches and chill overnight.

YIELDS 6 SERVINGS

The blushing apricot and woolly peach
Hang on thy walls, that every child may reach.

BEN JONSON

Fall
and
Winter

fall and winter Breakfasts

....

Sing a song of Seasons!
Something bright in all!
Flowers in the summer,
Fires in the Fall.

Robert Louis Stevenson

Being eternally optimistic, I keep all the Inn's wicker chairs and tables on
the terrace until early November, hoping for those occasional crisp and sunny au-
tumn days when we can still serve breakfast outside. And there are those guests
who feel the same way, happy to enjoy the autumnal morning sunshine. But, of
course, winter is undeniably on its way. Low shafts of sunlight stream through the
breakfast room windows, creating a marvelously diffused glow.

Now is the time when leaves cover the lawns, fresh flowers become a rarity
and, since I don't want dried flowers at the Inn, I go out hunting for whatever na-

ture has left. Bittersweet bushes push out a variety of colorful berries that become centerpieces in our living room. From the garden we pick winter asters of deep, earthy hues. We have hydrangeas and miniature pink and yellow mums and, throughout the winter, the Inn is scented with pine boughs, cinnamon, and logs burning in the fireplaces.

Earlier in the season is apple-picking time, which I adore. Tangerines, oranges, grapefruits, all the citrus fruits come into their own and that, to me, is a sure sign that the winter holidays are heading our way.

It's also a time when our appetites seem to grow.

As in the spring and summer, our menus change weekly. We still bake a glazed ham each Friday that lasts through the weekend, but the rest of the breakfast menu becomes more substantial. And, as winter descends, breakfasts become an even more important part of the day. Our guests bundle up after their morning meals and search out their favorite shops, spend their days antique hunting, visiting the art galleries or their families and friends.

Many of the recipes I've assembled here can be prepared the night before, which makes life a lot easier. Often, all that is required the following morning is for the cook to grill some bacon or sausages or slice up the ham. The muffins are so easy to make that once you've tried them, the whole procedure will become almost second nature. How gratifying it is to produce a basket of freshly made scones or muffins, with a dish of homemade marmalade on the side.

From a savory Potato Frittata served with a bowl of cut-up fruit, to delicious Orange French Toast—all are easy to make and satisfy the appetites that cold weather brings.

Breakfast should be unhurried and gracious and, therefore, the atmosphere also becomes essential. We always have the fires lit and, as in the other seasons, soft *music playing. There are sweet rolls or a coffeecake baking in the oven, flowers on all the tables, the usual array of newspapers for browsing, plenty of freshly brewed coffee, seasonal fruits in pretty bowls throughout, and a menu that we hope will brighten anyone's day.*

All happiness depends on a leisurely breakfast.

JOHN GUNTHER

Sourdough apple pancakes

My grandchildren love to help make these pancakes. With yeast in the recipe, they can watch the batter grow in front of their eyes. It's the yeast that gives the pancakes a sourdough taste. The batter can also be prepared the night before, covered tightly in plastic wrap, and kept in the refrigerator until morning.

> 4 tablespoons (½ stick) melted butter
> 1⅓ cups lukewarm milk (about 110°F.)
> 1 tablespoon dry yeast
> 1 tablespoon granulated sugar
> 1¾ cups flour
> 3 eggs
> ½ cup raisins
> 2 large apples (about 1 pound), peeled and grated
> 4 tablespoons clarified butter or safflower oil for sautéing
> Confectioners' sugar for dusting

In a mixing bowl, using a wooden spoon, beat together the butter, milk, yeast, sugar, flour, and eggs for about 5 minutes, until the batter is smooth and silky. Fold in the raisins and apples. Cover the bowl with a towel and let the batter rest in a warm place for 25 minutes to 1 hour, until the mixture rises.

Drop the batter from a ¼-cup measure onto a lightly buttered cast-iron skillet placed over medium-high heat. Turn the pancakes when bubbles appear in the center, and continue to cook until they are nicely brown on both sides.

Transfer the cooked pancakes to a platter and keep them warm in a 250°F. oven until all the batter has been used. Serve with a dusting of confectioners' sugar.

YIELDS EIGHTEEN 4-INCH PANCAKES

We serve these with thick slices of Virginia ham, turkey patties, or sausages. In winter, we add slices of ripe melon or sweet pineapple. In summer, we sprinkle fresh berries over the top.

Orange french toast

My mother used to buy fresh bakery rolls delivered in the morning by bicycle. Left-overs were made into French toast. The German word is Arme Ritter, *which, translated, means "poor royalty," odd since for me this is one of the more perfect breakfasts. We serve this on Sunday mornings with strips of crisp bacon or with the newer types of sausage: chicken, turkey, or veal. While the sausages sizzle on the griddle, we prepare the following ingredients, which takes about a half hour.*

> **4 eggs**
> **$^1/_4$ teaspoon salt**
> **1 teaspoon vanilla extract**
> **Grated rind of 1 orange**
> **$^3/_4$ cup freshly squeezed orange juice**
> **1 loaf French bread (16 inches long)**
> **3 tablespoons clarified butter**
> **$^1/_3$ cup confectioners' sugar**
> **2 orange slices, for garnish**

In a bowl, beat the eggs with a fork until smooth. Add the salt, vanilla, and grated orange rind and juice. Stir to blend. Pour the mixture into a shallow casserole large enough to fit all the bread slices in one layer.

Cut the bread diagonally into 8 to 10 slices. Each slice should be about 7 inches long. Place the sliced bread over the eggs in the casserole dish. Let stand for about 30 minutes, turning the slices once, halfway through the soaking time.

Spoon 2 tablespoons of clarified butter into a heavy skillet and heat to medium-hot. Add as many bread slices as the skillet can hold without crowding. Sauté the bread on both sides until they're done, 6 or 7 minutes total. Repeat with the remaining bread slices, adding more butter as needed.

Dust with confectioners' sugar and serve with slices of orange.

This can be put together
the night before. Day-old
plain white bread, or day-
old brioche also make
excellent toast. Prepare
the bread as described in
the recipe, pour the egg
mixture into a shallow
casserole, add the bread
slices, cover with plastic
wrap, and place in the
refrigerator until
morning.

Fruit and yogurt drink

A fresh fruit drink is what so many of us crave in the dead of winter. This one is delicious, substantial, and low in fat. A great pick-me-up for any time of day.

> *8 dried apricots, preferably California-grown*
> *¼ cup sugar*
> *1 cup water*
> *1 banana, peeled*
> *1 cup ripe golden pineapple chunks*
> *1 cup nonfat plain yogurt*
> *5 ice cubes*

Place the apricots, sugar, and water in a saucepan and bring to a boil. Lower the heat, cover, and simmer for 10 minutes. Set aside to cool.

Pour the apricot mixture into a blender, add the rest of the ingredients, and blend at high speed until smooth.

YIELDS FOUR 8-OUNCE SERVINGS

This is a versatile drink that can be adjusted to suit your taste. For a rich, darker beverage, substitute 8 prunes for the apricots. You can also try replacing the pineapple with oranges or ripe pears, which are especially good. When in season, mangoes and papayas give this cooler that special tropical taste. Just remember that with any substitution the same quantities are always used.

Potato frittata

A fabulous combination of savory, sweet, and creamy. We serve this with orange slices, a bowl of sour cream, and a basket of black bread. In summer, we substitute ripe papayas for the oranges. Try using a heavy cast-iron skillet. It not only looks wonderful when serving up this dish, but it cooks better, too.

6 strips of bacon
2 tablespoons olive oil
2 baking potatoes (about 1 pound), peeled and sliced thin
$1^1/_2$ teaspoons salt
2 medium onions, finely chopped (2 cups)
2 garlic cloves, minced (1 tablespoon)
3 ounces cream cheese, cut into small cubes
2 plum tomatoes, sliced
4 eggs
$^1/_3$ cup cream
$^2/_3$ cup milk
$^1/_8$ teaspoon cayenne
$^1/_4$ cup freshly grated Parmesan cheese

Preheat the oven to 375°F.

In a heavy 10-inch skillet with 2-inch sides, sauté the bacon until the strips are crisp and browned. Transfer the bacon to a plate and discard the fat in the pan. In the same skillet, heat the olive oil. Add the potatoes and sprinkle them with the salt. Scatter the onions and garlic on top. Cover the skillet and, stirring twice, sauté the vegetables over a medium heat until soft, about 10 minutes. Crumble the bacon over the mixture, add the cream cheese, and top with the tomato slices. Press down on the mixture, spreading it evenly into the skillet.

Beat together the eggs, cream, milk, and cayenne. Pour the eggs evenly over the mixture in the skillet. Sprinkle with the Parmesan and bake, uncovered, for 40 minutes or until the frittata is set, puffed, and nicely browned. Remove the frittata from the oven and let it set for 10 minutes. Cut into wedges and serve.

Yields 4 to 6 servings

If you want to serve this as a luncheon meal, double the ingredients and use a casserole that can go from stovetop to oven to table. Leftovers, if any, can be served at breakfast the next day. Reheat, uncovered, in a preheated 375°F. oven for 10 minutes.

Sliced potatoes
with sour cream and caviar

A royal way to treat the humble potato and create a special breakfast or a delightful addition to any buffet.

> **2 pounds small baking potatoes**
> **3/4 cup sour cream**
> **4 ounces fresh salmon caviar**
> **2 tablespoons chopped fresh chives**

In a pot of water, boil the potatoes in their skins until they're tender. Drain, peel, and slice while they're still warm.

Mound the sour cream in the middle of a large serving platter. Create a bed in the center and fill it with caviar. Ring the platter with the potato slices. Sprinkle with the chives.

YIELDS 6 SERVINGS

Honey-almond granola

~

We've sold this granola at Loaves and Fishes for going on 18 years, and we now serve this popular breakfast treat year-round at the Inn, with sliced bananas in the colder months and fresh berries when the seasons turn warmer.

4 cups rolled oats
2 cups sliced almonds
1 teaspoon ground cardamom
$^1/_2$ cup honey
$^1/_4$ cup peanut oil
1 cup raisins

Preheat the oven to 300°F.

Place the oats, almonds, and cardamom in a bowl and toss lightly. Heat the honey and peanut oil in a small saucepan until they're a little more than warm but not boiling. The mixture should be runny. Pour the honey and oil over the oat mixture and toss well to coat thoroughly. Spread the mixture on a baking sheet and bake for 30 minutes, or until golden brown.

Remove from the oven and stir in the raisins. Let the mixture cool to room temperature.

~

YIELDS 7 CUPS

STORED IN AN AIRTIGHT
CONTAINER, AND KEPT IN A
COOL PLACE, THE GRANOLA
WILL KEEP FOR UP TO
4 WEEKS.

Salmon with soft-boiled eggs and caramelized vegetables

An untraditional dish that is either a morning feast or a satisfying lunch, we serve this to our guests with toasted bagels and cream cheese.

4 cups 1-inch cubed, peeled butternut squash
2 cups 1-inch cubed, peeled celery root
6 cups 1-inch cubed, peeled potatoes, preferably Yukon Gold
2 cups 1-inch cubed, peeled fennel bulbs
2 cups 1-inch cubed, peeled onions
$^1/_2$ cup good olive oil
1 tablespoon kosher salt
$^1/_2$ pound sliced smoked salmon
4 eggs, soft-boiled (see box)
2 tablespoons chopped fresh dill or parsley

Preheat the oven to 450°F.

Place the vegetables in a bowl. Stir in the olive oil and salt. Spread the oil-coated vegetables in one layer onto 2 large baking sheets. Roast for 35 to 40 minutes, until all the vegetables are tender and light brown.

Distribute the vegetables onto 4 heated dinner plates. Place 2 salmon slices on each plate. Place a soft-boiled egg on top of the vegetables, slicing the top so the yellow runs. Sprinkle with chopped dill or parsley.

YIELDS 4 SERVINGS

To make perfect soft-boiled eggs, place the eggs in a pan of cold water. Bring the water to a boil over high heat. Lower the heat and simmer the eggs for 2 minutes (or to your taste). Drain and quickly run them under cold water to stop the cooking process while the eggs stay hot.

For a different taste treat, substitute sweet potato for the traditional white potato, or try any other kind of squash or zucchini. The vegetables can be cut the day before and refrigerated, covered, in an airtight container until morning.

We serve this for lunch with a salad of arugula, endive, and lots of parsley. Peel and thinly slice 3 lemons. Add the lemons to the salad. Toss with olive oil and lemon juice. Or try serving this with chilled green grapes tossed into a salad of greens.

Wienerbrot
(danish coffee bread strips)

The beauty of this recipe is that you can put it all together the night before, refrigerate it, then bake it in the morning while you're frying up some eggs and ham. We serve the whole loaf on a board, sliced and ready to eat. It turns a simple breakfast into a unique treat.

> *3 tablespoons warm water (110°F.)*
> *1 tablespoon dry yeast*
> *12 tablespoons (1½ sticks) softened butter*
> *2 tablespoons plus ½ cup granulated sugar*
> *3 eggs*
> *2¾ cups flour*
> *½ teaspoon salt*
> *¾ cup water*
> *12 ounces (about 2 cups) pitted prunes*
> *5½ tablespoons fresh lemon juice*
> *½ teaspoon ground cinnamon*
> *1½ cups confectioners' sugar*

In a small cup, mix together the water and yeast. Let the mixture stand for about 5 minutes to dissolve the yeast.

Using an electric mixer, beat together the butter and 2 tablespoons of sugar until they're creamy. Add the eggs and beat until they blend with the butter. Add the flour, salt, and yeast mixture. Beat at low speed for about 5 minutes, scraping down the sides twice.

Gather the dough into a ball and place it in a lightly buttered mixing bowl. Turn the dough once, then cover the bowl with a kitchen towel and place it in a warm place for approximately 1½ hours to allow the dough to rise.

Preheat the oven to 375°F. Butter a baking sheet.

In a covered pan, combine the $^3/_4$ cup of water, $^1/_2$ cup of sugar, and the prunes. Cook for about 10 minutes. Cool slightly, then puree in a food processor, adding 1$^1/_2$ tablespoons of the lemon juice and the cinnamon until the consistency is partly smooth, partly chunky.

Roll out half the dough on a floured surface to a 12-by-12-inch square. Spread the dough with half the prune mixture. Roll the dough loosely into a jelly roll and transfer it to the baking sheet. Repeat the same procedure with the remaining half of the dough and prune spread. Flatten both strips with a rolling pin until they are about $^3/_4$ inch thick. Bake for 20 to 25 minutes, or until golden brown. Remove from the oven and cool slightly.

With a fork, beat together the confectioners' sugar and remaining 4 tablespoons of lemon juice. Drizzle the glaze over the Danish coffee strips while they're still slightly warm.

YIELDS 6 SERVINGS

INSTEAD OF PRUNES, MIX TOGETHER: $^1/_4$ CUP RAISINS; $^1/_2$ CUP CHOPPED WALNUTS; $^1/_2$ CUP SUGAR; 1 TEASPOON GROUND CINNAMON. OR TRY SPREADING PRESERVES, SUCH AS APRICOT, STRAWBERRY, RASPBERRY, OR A DELICIOUS PLUM JAM OVER THE DOUGH BEFORE BAKING. USE 1$^1/_2$ CUPS PER STRIP.

(continued)

To prepare this the night before, mix the dough ingredients, place the dough in a clean bowl, and cover tightly with plastic wrap so the mixture doesn't rise and run over the edges. In the morning, uncover and allow the dough to warm to room temperature, then proceed as directed. If you have time to make and bake the bread the day before, make sure you wrap it in foil after it's cooled. The next morning, place it in a preheated 375°F. oven for 10 minutes, unwrapped.

Freeze leftovers in tightly wrapped foil. When ready to reheat, place the wrapped, frozen bread strips in a preheated 375°F. oven for 30 minutes.

Scones

These delicious little bread cakes have always been a favorite at Loaves and Fishes. At the Inn we serve them with scrambled eggs, crisp bacon, butter, and fresh marmalade, or tucked inside a basket of sweet rolls as part of our Continental Breakfast. These take very little time to make.

3 cups flour
¹/₄ cup plus 3 tablespoons sugar
2 teaspoons baking powder
8 tablespoons (1 stick) margarine, cut into 8 slices
4 tablespoons (¹/₂ stick) butter, cut into 4 slices
2 eggs
³/₄ cup milk
¹/₂ cup raisins
2 teaspoons fresh lemon juice
1 egg yolk
1 tablespoon heavy cream

Preheat the oven to 375°F. Butter a baking sheet.

Place the flour, ¹/₄ cup sugar, and the baking powder in the bowl of an electric mixer. Add the margarine and butter and mix at low speed until the mixture appears crumbly. Add the eggs, milk, raisins, and lemon juice. Mix at low speed until the dough sticks together.

Transfer the dough to a countertop and pat the dough down to a 1-inch thickness. Cut the dough into triangles or 3-inch rounds. Place the scones on the baking sheet, keeping them about 2 inches apart.

In a small bowl, beat the egg yolk and cream until they're blended. Brush the mixture over the top of each scone. Sprinkle with the remaining 3 tablespoons of sugar and bake for 25 minutes, or until the scones are golden brown.

(continued)

YIELDS 12 SCONES

....

FOR A VARIATION

ADD A TEASPOON OF
CINNAMON TO THE 3
TABLESPOONS OF SUGAR FOR
SPRINKLING OVER THE
SCONES. YOU CAN ALSO
SUBSTITUTE A VARIETY OF
DRIED BERRIES, SUCH AS
CRANBERRIES, CHERRIES, OR
SULTANAS FOR THE RAISINS.
THE LEFTOVER SCONES
SHOULD BE KEPT IN AN
AIRTIGHT CONTAINER. OR, IF
FROZEN, WRAPPED IN FOIL. TO
REHEAT, PLACE THEM, STILL
FOIL-WRAPPED, IN A
PREHEATED 375°F. OVEN FOR
20 MINUTES.

....

Orange marmalade

A Loaves and Fishes shelf item for 18 years that now shares equal popularity at our breakfasts at the Inn.

 4 large or 5 medium seedless oranges
 2 lemons
 8 cups water
 8 cups sugar

Cut the oranges and lemons in half crosswise, then into paper-thin slices. Place the sliced fruit in a large stainless-steel saucepan. Add the water. Stirring often, bring to a boil. Remove from the heat and stir in the sugar until it is dissolved. Let stand overnight at room temperature.

The next day, bring the mixture back to a boil. Lower the heat and simmer, uncovered, for about 2 hours. Turn up the heat and boil rapidly, stirring often, for 30 minutes. Transfer the marmalade to seven 8-ounce hot, clean jars. Seal with lids and store in a cool place. The marmalade will keep for up to 3 months.

YIELDS 7 CUPS

Pear and walnut muffins

Another addition to our Continental Breakfast basket of sweet rolls. We also offer these muffins, warmed, with cream cheese on the side, along with a full breakfast of eggs and bacon. They are mouthwateringly good and take only minutes to make.

$2^1/_3$ cups flour
2 teaspoons baking powder
$^1/_2$ teaspoon baking soda
1 cup granulated sugar
$^1/_4$ teaspoon salt
1 teaspoon ground cinnamon
1 teaspoon ground cardamom
2 small eggs
$^3/_4$ cup milk
12 tablespoons ($1^1/_2$ sticks) melted and cooled butter
1 cup peeled and coarsely chopped ripe pear
$^1/_2$ cup coarsely chopped walnuts

THE TOPPING

$^1/_2$ cup light brown sugar
$^1/_2$ teaspoon ground cardamom
$^1/_2$ teaspoon ground cinnamon
4 tablespoons ($^1/_4$ cup) cold butter, cut into small pieces

Preheat the oven to 400°F. Line a 12-cup muffin tin with paper liners.

Place 2 cups of the flour, the baking powder, baking soda, sugar, salt, cinnamon, and cardamom in a mixing bowl and stir to blend. Add the eggs, milk, and melted butter. Stir with a wooden spoon, mixing the ingredients together.

Don't overbeat. A few lumps in the batter are fine. Add the chopped pear and the walnuts. Stir to blend. Spoon the mixture into the muffin tin.

For the topping, in a small bowl, combine the ingredients and mix with your hands until the batter is crumbly. Scatter the crumbs evenly over the 12 muffins. Bake for 20 to 25 minutes, or until a toothpick inserted in the center of a muffin comes out clean. Serve warm or at room temperature.

YIELDS 12 MUFFINS

THESE MUFFINS SHOULD NOT BE REFRIGERATED. STORE LEFTOVERS IN TIGHTLY WRAPPED FOIL OR IN AN AIRTIGHT CONTAINER AND KEEP THEM AT ROOM TEMPERATURE. OR FREEZE THEM. WHEN REHEATING, TAKE THEM FROM THE FREEZER AND PLACE THEM, STILL WRAPPED, IN A PREHEATED 375°F. OVEN FOR 30 MINUTES.

Crumb-topped coffeecake

A traditional coffeecake that is great at breakfast, brunch, lunch, tea, or with ice cream as a dessert.

8 tablespoons (1 stick) softened butter
1 cup granulated sugar
3 eggs
1 teaspoon vanilla extract
2 cups flour
1 teaspoon baking powder
1 teaspoon baking soda
1 cup sour cream

CRUMB TOPPING

1 cup light brown sugar
1 teaspoon ground cinnamon
1 tablespoon flour
1 cup coarsely chopped walnuts
4 tablespoons (1/2 stick) butter

Preheat the oven to 350°F. Butter a 13-by-9-by-2-inch baking pan.

In the bowl of an electric mixer, beat the butter and sugar at medium speed until creamy. Add the eggs and vanilla. Mix well to combine. Add the flour, baking powder, baking soda, and sour cream. At low speed, mix until the batter is smooth. Spoon the batter into the baking pan, spreading the batter evenly.

To make the topping, combine all the ingredients in a small bowl and, with your hands, work until they're crumbly. Sprinkle over the batter.

Bake for 40 to 45 minutes, or until a toothpick inserted in the center comes out clean. Serve warm or at room temperature.

YIELDS 12 SERVINGS OR 1 CAKE

WHEN FRESH BLUEBERRIES
ARE IN SEASON, WE ADD
2 CUPS AS A LAST
INGREDIENT AND GENTLY
FOLD THEM INTO THE
BATTER BY HAND. IDEALLY,
THIS CAKE SHOULD BE
EATEN THE DAY IT IS MADE.
WE FIND IT USUALLY IS.

Stewed prunes

※

We make this recipe once a week at the Inn. It keeps very well when refrigerated. If serving this as a dessert, use port wine instead of apple juice and substitute 1 vanilla bean for the cinnamon stick.

> *12 ounces (about 2 cups) pitted prunes*
> *³/₄ cup sugar*
> *1 cup apple juice*
> *1 cup water*
> *1 cinnamon stick*

Place all the ingredients in a saucepan and bring to a boil. Lower the heat and simmer, uncovered, for 10 minutes. Chill, covered, overnight. Serve the prunes in a glass dish with a little cream on the side.

※

YIELDS 6 SERVINGS

Salads
for fall and winter

According to the Spanish Proverb, four persons are wanted
to make a good salad: a spendthrift for oil, a miser for vinegar,
a counselor for salt, and a madman to stir it all up.

ABRAHAM HAYWARD

Fall and winter salads feature greens that are much sturdier than those of
spring and summer and therefore are capable of standing up to heartier dressings.
It's the time of year when we top our salads with thin shavings of Parmesan or
marble the tops with crumbs of tasty Gorgonzola. Curly heads of frisée, endives,
and romaine lettuces take the place of summer's tender, leafy greens. Cabbages are
in season, as are apples, pears, and oranges. In our markets, the bins seem to be
brimming over with potatoes, root vegetables, bunches of nutritious and vibrant
beets. We have celeriac and fennel bulbs galore and an astonishing assortment of
nuts that seem to find their way into almost all our cooking.

The most amazing salads can be created by even the most frugal of cooks. Vegetables, fish, meats, leftovers from last night's dinner suddenly reappear disguised in a salad. A solitary apple can add just the right amount of sweetness and crunch to make an ordinary salad something special. Left-over potatoes get sliced, dressed with vinaigrette, sprinkled with herbs, and make their entrance as a perfect complement to a lunch of sandwiches or soup.

Some of our salad and sandwich recipes stand up as meals on their own, such as our Steak Salad, Pan Bagnat, or Lavash Roll-Up Sandwiches. Our salad of Blood Orange, Onion, and Green Olives would be perfect to precede a rich dinner of Roast Goose, Braised Pheasant, or Rabbit. It is extremely refreshing, and the variety of flavors, both savory and juicy sweet, seem to prepare the palate for what's to come. Celeriac Salad goes with almost any main course, but it can also be served as a starter for a substantial soup. Our Cabbage, Fennel, and Apple Slaw is perfect with Baked Ham, Roast Duck, and Beef Ragout.

We hope that we offer a varied selection of recipes that are interesting, sometimes unusual but always delicious alternatives to what one normally would expect of "a salad."

Steak salad with roasted peppers on frisée

❧

Served with French baguettes or sourdough ficelle, this makes a fabulous lunch or a light supper.

3 pounds ³/₄-inch-thick sirloin, T-bone, or Porterhouse,
    fat removed

THE MARINADE

3 tablespoons olive oil
2 tablespoons toasted sesame oil
2 tablespoons dark brown sugar
3 tablespoons soy sauce
3 tablespoons sherry vinegar
1 tablespoon fresh lemon juice
1 tablespoon peeled and minced fresh ginger
3 garlic cloves, minced
1 teaspoon hot pepper flakes

THE VEGETABLES

1 red bell pepper
1 yellow bell pepper
1 red onion, thinly sliced
2 tablespoons olive oil
¹/₄ pound frisée, roots discarded

The dressing

2 tablespoons sherry vinegar
2 tablespoons soy sauce
2 tablespoons toasted sesame oil
1 teaspoon granulated sugar

Place the steak in a glass dish.

Combine all the marinade ingredients in the bowl of a food processor and pulse until smooth. Pour the mixture over the steak and let it stand at room temperature for 30 minutes. Preheat the broiler for 10 minutes. Transfer the steaks to a sheet pan and discard the marinade. Broil the steaks for 3 to 4 minutes on each side. Remove from the oven and set aside.

Reduce the oven temperature to 425°.

For the vegetables, core and cut each pepper into 8 strips. Place them in the roasting pan with the onion slices. Drizzle with the oil and roast for 30 minutes. Remove from the oven and set aside.

Divide the frisée among 4 dinner plates. Slice the steak into $1/2$-inch strips and mound it on the frisée. Arrange the roasted vegetables around the sliced steak.

In a bowl, whisk together all the dressing ingredients and spoon some over each salad.

YIELDS 4 SERVINGS

Beetroot salad with fresh rosemary

Try sprinkling shaved Parmesan or crumbled Stilton over the beets—it's delicious.

> 8 medium beets, each about 1½ inches in diameter
> ½ cup thinly sliced onion rings
> ¼ cup olive oil
> ¼ cup balsamic vinegar
> ¾ teaspoon salt
> ¼ teaspoon freshly ground black pepper
> 1 tablespoon finely minced fresh rosemary leaves
> 1 bunch curly chicory
> ¼ cup toasted walnuts

Preheat the oven to 400°F.

Place the unpeeled beets in a small roasting pan. Cover tightly with foil and bake for 1 hour and 15 minutes. Remove from the oven and cool.

Peel and slice the beets. Place them in a bowl. Add the onion. In a small container with a tight-fitting lid, shake together the olive oil, vinegar, salt, and pepper. Pour half the dressing over the beets. Add the rosemary and mix gently. Using the inner leaves only, cut the chicory into coarsely julienned slices. Toss with the remaining dressing and divide among 4 serving plates.

Mound the beets on top of the dressed chicory and sprinkle each salad with toasted walnuts.

YIELDS 4 SERVINGS

Celeriac salad

A crunchy, tangy, and refreshing salad.

> *1 large or 2 medium celeriac (celery root)*
> *Juice of 1/2 lemon*
> *1 teaspoon salt*
> *1/2 teaspoon freshly ground black pepper*
> *2/3 cup mayonnaise*
> *3 tablespoons grainy mustard*
> *1 tablespoon white wine vinegar*
> *3 tablespoons heavy cream*
> *1/4 cup olive oil*
> *1/3 cup finely chopped fresh flat-leaf parsley*
> *1/3 cup finely chopped scallions, green part only*

Peel the celeriac and cut it into chunks. Using a food processor with the shredding disc in place, shred the celeriac into fine sticks. Place in a bowl and toss with the lemon juice, salt, and pepper.

Place the mayonnaise, mustard, vinegar, cream, and oil in a small bowl. Whisk until combined. It should be smooth and creamy. Pour the dressing over the celeriac, add the parsley and scallion greens, and fold to blend.

YIELDS 4 TO 6 SERVINGS

Lentil, pear, and romaine salad

This is a very popular first course that we often serve at our Inn.

1 cup apple juice
3 cups water
1 cup lentils
3 garlic cloves, peeled
1 large white onion, cut in half
$^1/_2$ red onion
1 ripe green pear
$1^1/_2$ cups thinly sliced celery
1 small head romaine lettuce
$^1/_2$ cup toasted pecan halves

THE DRESSING

3 tablespoons red wine vinegar
$^1/_4$ cup olive oil
$^3/_4$ teaspoon salt
$^1/_2$ teaspoon freshly ground black pepper

Pour the apple juice and water into a large pot, add the lentils, garlic, and white onion and cook, covered, over a medium heat for 35 minutes. Drain the lentils, discarding the garlic and onion. Set the lentils aside to cool a bit, then place them in a large bowl.

Cut the red onion into thin slices, and separate the slices into rings. Cut the pear in half, remove the core, and cut the pear into thin slices. Add the onion rings, pear slices, and celery to the lentils. Cut the romaine lettuce into bite-size pieces. Add to the lentil mixture. Add the pecans.

For the dressing, combine the ingredients in a jar with a tight-fitting lid and shake well. Pour the dressing over the lentil salad and mix well. Taste for seasoning. Serve warm.

Yields 4 servings

LENTILLES DU PUY ARE THE BEST SINCE THEY KEEP THEIR SHAPE WHILE COOKING. YOU'LL FIND THEM AT MOST SPECIALTY FOOD STORES.

TO DOUBLE THIS RECIPE, INCREASE THE APPLE JUICE TO 1½ CUPS AND THE WATER TO 4 CUPS. IF USING 2 CUPS OF LENTILS, THE DRESSING INGREDIENTS SHOULD BE INCREASED TO 1½ TIMES THE RECIPE.

Cabbage, fennel, and apple slaw

One of my favorites, this stands up to almost any grilled meat. Using fennel instead of the traditional celery gives this slaw an exotic, excellent flavor.

> 1 small head white cabbage
> 1 fennel bulb, stalks and fronds removed
> 1 tart apple, halved, cored, cut into thin slices
> $1/3$ cup rice vinegar
> $1/3$ cup safflower oil
> $1^1/2$ teaspoons sugar
> 1 teaspoon salt
> 2 tablespoons soy sauce
> 2 teaspoons toasted sesame oil

Using the slicing disc of your food processor, shred the cabbage and fennel. If doing this by hand, cut the vegetables as fine as possible. Place the shredded cabbage and fennel in a large bowl. Add the sliced apples.

Combine the remaining ingredients in a container with a tight-fitting lid. Shake hard to blend well. Pour the dressing over the vegetables. Toss to blend.

YIELDS 6 SERVINGS

SERVE THE SLAW WITHIN
2 HOURS OF PREPARATION,
OTHERWISE IT WILL RELEASE
ITS JUICES AND LOSE
ITS CRISPNESS.

Lavash Roll-up Sandwiches
Cabbage, Fennel, and Apple Slaw
Peanut Cookies

Rabbit Braised in Wine, Onions, Mushrooms, and Herbs (on right)

Leeks au Gratin

Roast Turkey with Apple, Orange, and Raisin Stuffing

Chanterelles, Shallots, and Peas

Butternut Squash Puree with Fresh Ginger

Cranberry-Pear Sauce

Hazelnut Trifle

Blood orange, onion, and green olive salad

※

Blood oranges are available from December through March and are at their best in January and February. If you cannot find any, you can substitute any sweet juicy orange.

4 blood oranges
1 red onion
¹/₂ cup drained green olives in brine
¹/₂ teaspoon salt
2 teaspoons coarsely cracked black peppercorns
¹/₄ cup good-quality olive oil

Peel the oranges as you would an apple. Remove the pits and white pith. Cut the oranges into ¹/₄-inch rounds and arrange them on 4 salad plates. Slice the onion into paper-thin rings. Divide among the plates. Pit and slice the olives and scatter them over the oranges and onions. Sprinkle with salt and peppercorns. Drizzle 1 tablespoon of olive oil over each salad and serve.

※

YIELDS 4 SERVINGS

Frisée and endive salad with toasted walnuts

❧

1 small head frisée lettuce
1 Belgian endive
1 teaspoon Dijon mustard
1^1/$_2$ tablespoons red wine vinegar
3 tablespoons olive oil
^{1}/$_2$ teaspoon salt
^{1}/$_4$ teaspoon freshly ground black pepper
^{1}/$_2$ cup toasted walnut halves

Cut the frisée and endive into bite-size pieces and arrange in a glass bowl. Combine the mustard, vinegar, olive oil, salt, and pepper in a jar with a tight-fitting lid and shake well.

Sprinkle the walnuts over the greens and pour the dressing over all. Toss lightly and serve.

❧

YIELDS 4 SERVINGS

Pan bagnat

Loosely translated, this is a salade niçoise sandwich. Make it ahead of time and wrap it so that all the flavors have a chance to mingle. It makes an excellent, fully satisfying, and perfect take-out lunch.

> *2 red bell peppers, cut in half*
> *2 garlic cloves*
> *1 teaspoon salt*
> *¹/₄ cup olive oil*
> *4 hard rolls, halved, not separated, with some of the insides removed*
> *8 romaine lettuce leaves*
> *1 small red onion, cut into thin slices*
> *4 eggs, hard-boiled, shelled, and sliced*
> *8 black olives, pitted and sliced*
> *8 anchovy fillets*
> *2 tablespoons drained capers*
> *¹/₂ teaspoon fresh lemon juice*

Preheat the oven to 425°F.

Place the peppers on a sheet pan and roast them for 30 minutes. Set aside. Mash the garlic and salt together to make a paste. Place the paste in a bowl and add the olive oil. Brush a little of the mixture onto the bottom half of each roll. Layer each roll with 1 lettuce leaf, ¹/₂ red pepper, some onion rings, 1 sliced egg, 2 sliced olives, 2 anchovy fillets, and a sprinkling of capers. Top with the remaining lettuce leaves. Add the lemon juice to the remaining garlic-oil and drizzle over each sandwich. Close the roll and cover the sandwiches in plastic wrap until ready to serve.

YIELDS 4 SANDWICHES

Lavash roll-up sandwiches

We make loads of these sandwiches for fall picnics or for guests who plan a day of bicycling to the shops and beaches. You can try many combinations: mayonnaise, smoked chicken breasts, sliced avocado, tomatoes, and cheddar cheese; or cream cheese, smoked salmon, and cucumber.

3 red bell peppers
One 12-by-24-inch sheet of lavash bread
$^1/_3$ cup mayonnaise
$^1/_3$ cup honey mustard
$^1/_2$ pound mozzarella cheese, sliced
$^1/_2$ pound turkey breast, sliced
$^1/_2$ teaspoon salt
$^1/_3$ teaspoon freshly ground black pepper
3 cups arugula leaves

Preheat the oven to 400°F.

Core and halve the peppers. Remove and discard the seeds. Place the peppers on a baking sheet and roast them for 30 minutes, until soft. Set aside.

Open the lavash bread on a work surface, with the long side facing you. Combine the mayonnaise and honey mustard and spread it over the flatbread. Lay the mozzarella slices in a row, about 4 inches from the edge of the bread nearest you. Top with the roasted peppers. Arrange the turkey slices over the peppers and sprinkle with salt and pepper. Top with the arugula leaves.

Starting at the filling end, lightly roll the bread, jelly-roll fashion, tucking the filling under as you go. Cut into 6 equal pieces. Wrap in plastic wrap until ready to serve. These sandwiches are best when consumed within 6 hours of preparation.

YIELDS 6 ROLL-UP SANDWICHES

···

LAVASH BREAD IS
AVAILABLE IN SPECIALTY
FOOD STORES OR IN THE
DELI SECTION OF YOUR
SUPERMARKET.

···

Starters
for fall and winter

Fan the sinking flame of hilarity with the wing of friendship;
and pass the rosy wine.

CHARLES DICKENS

*T*he advent of the winter holiday season brings with it a swirl of exhilarating cocktail parties and lush dinners. This is when the Inn seems to sing. Branches of bittersweet spread majestically from the large vases that we place around the living room. Their red berries open slightly to reveal a beautiful interior orange hull. It's the time when we decide where to arrange the pine boughs and where the Christmas tree would look best. We start to untangle yards of Christmas lights to string outside and in. The excitement is almost palpable.

Innumerable parties seem to materialize all throughout November and into the New Year, truly festive times when menus are planned with great care. Although this is definitely the busiest of times, I somehow never feel tired; in fact, I feel mysteriously energized.

When considering the list of starters for a fall or winter cocktail party or buffet, we begin by choosing foods with tastes that are both unique and complementary. They must be easy to handle and, equally important, there should be enough to go around, though not too much. Starters are meant to enliven the palate, not to stifle the appetite.

Most of the assembled recipes, particularly the Curried Scallops, the pâtés, and our Shrimp in Sesame Dressing, are ideal as party starters and excellent as first courses. The Wild Mushroom and Onion Tart is great for breakfast, or it can be served as a light lunch with salad or soups.

Thank goodness I have a husband who shares my enthusiasms. He has traveled throughout the world with me, patiently waiting as I huddled over my notebooks, trying to capture the essence of some new and marvelous food we had just tasted. Once we returned home, I set to work in the kitchen trying to re-create those recipes that particularly excited me.

Here are some of them.

Wald pilze und zwiebel kuchen

A *Wild Mushroom and Onion Tart* that can serve as a fulfilling breakfast or a delectable addition to your buffet. We have also served it as a light lunch with a salad of winter greens drizzled with lemony vinaigrette.

THE CRUST

1^1/$_2$ cups flour
8 tablespoons (1 stick) cold butter, cut into 8 pieces
^{1}/$_4$ teaspoon salt
1 egg yolk
3 tablespoons cold water

THE FILLING

1 tablespoon olive oil
1^1/$_2$ cups finely chopped white onions
1 tablespoon butter
4 cups coarsely chopped wild mushrooms (Portobellos
    or crimini)
1^1/$_2$ teaspoons salt
^{1}/$_4$ pound sharp cheddar cheese, grated (1 cup)
3 eggs
^{1}/$_2$ cup heavy cream
^{1}/$_2$ cup milk
^{1}/$_8$ teaspoon cayenne
^{1}/$_4$ cup freshly grated Parmesan cheese
1 tablespoon chopped fresh parsley

(continued)

To make the crust, place the flour, butter, and salt in the bowl of a food processor. Pulse until the butter is the size of peas. Add the egg yolk and water and pulse again until the dough starts to hold together. Transfer the dough to a lightly floured surface and quickly gather it into a ball. Cover with plastic wrap and chill for 30 minutes.

Preheat the oven to 375°F. Lightly butter a 10-inch quiche dish, $1^{1}/_{4}$ inches deep.

Roll out the dough on a floured surface into a 12-inch circle. Fit the dough into the quiche dish, pressing it lightly into the sides. Cover the un-cooked pastry shell with foil. Pour in dry beans or "blind baking pellets," to fill the pan. This method prevents the pastry shell from shrinking during its baking time. Bake for 15 minutes. Remove the beans and save them for another time. Discard the foil and bake the tart shell 5 minutes longer.

For the filling, using a heavy skillet, heat the olive oil and sauté the onions over low heat for 10 minutes, making sure the onions don't brown. Scrape the onions into the tart shell. In the same skillet, melt the butter and sauté the mushrooms over high heat, stirring often, until brown. Spoon the mushrooms over the onions. Sprinkle with the salt and cheddar cheese. In a bowl, beat the eggs into the cream, milk, and cayenne. Pour the mixture into the tart shell. Sprinkle with the Parmesan and parsley. Bake for 40 minutes, or until nicely browned.

YIELDS 6 SERVINGS AS A FIRST COURSE

Fresh salmon tartare cured in lemon and lime juice

For this recipe you should buy the freshest salmon available. Serve it with buttered slices of toasted grainy bread, crème fraîche, and salmon roe.

1½ pounds fresh salmon, finely chopped
¼ cup minced onion
1 garlic clove
½ teaspoon salt
2 tablespoons fresh lime juice
2 tablespoons fresh lemon juice
1½ tablespoons fine brandy
2 teaspoons Dijon mustard
2 tablespoons finely chopped fresh dill
2 tablespoons finely chopped fresh parsley
½ teaspoon freshly ground black pepper
¼ cup crème fraîche
¼ cup salmon roe
4 lemon wedges

In a bowl, combine all but the last 3 ingredients, and blend gently but thoroughly. Chill for 3 to 6 hours.

To serve, pile the salmon in the center of 4 plates. Top each mound with a dollop of crème fraîche and on top of that place a spoonful of salmon roe. Garnish with a lemon wedge and offer toasted bread on the side.

YIELDS 4 SERVINGS

Smoked salmon mousse platter

᷒

Not only is this sublime, it also makes a beautiful presentation; pink salmon surrounded by pale green cucumber rounds and dark grainy bread. An ideal dish to make the morning of your dinner party, or the night before. All you need to do is take it out of the refrigerator moments before your guests arrive, slice up the cucumbers and bread, and it's ready to serve.

¹/₂ pound smoked salmon
¹/₂ pound cream cheese
1¹/₂ tablespoons fresh lemon juice
1 cup sour cream
¹/₈ teaspoon cayenne
3 tablespoons drained capers
¹/₄ cup finely chopped scallion greens
1 seedless cucumber
5 thin slices dark, firm, grainy bread
Unsalted butter for spreading
¹/₂ cup finely chopped white onion
2 tablespoons chopped fresh dill

In a food processor, process the salmon for 8 seconds until it has a fine consistency. Add the cream cheese, lemon juice, sour cream, and cayenne, and process again until the mixture is well combined and smooth. Transfer to a bowl and fold in 2 tablespoons of the capers and the scallions. Chill the salmon mousse for 4 hours or overnight.

Pile the salmon mousse onto the center of a large platter. Slice the cucumber into ¹/₄-inch rounds and arrange them around the mousse. Butter the bread, then cut each slice into quarters. Place the small bread squares around the cucumbers, continuing until the platter is filled. Sprinkle the salmon mousse with the chopped onion, the remaining capers, and the dill. Cover with plastic wrap and refrigerate until ready to serve.

YIELDS 6 SERVINGS

ALTHOUGH THIS RECIPE ALLOWS FOR A GENEROUS SERVING FOR 6, YOU CAN ALSO SERVE IT AS A BUFFET LUNCH BY DOUBLING THE INGREDIENTS. AS A FINGER FOOD, SPOON DOLLOPS OF MOUSSE ON TINY RADICCHIO LEAVES AND ROLL THEM UP. WE ALSO SPOON PORTIONS ON ENDIVE LEAVES, WHICH LOOK QUITE BEAUTIFUL FANNED OVER A LARGE WHITE PLATTER. SMALL, DELICATE, AND DELICIOUS.

FOR BREAKFAST

OUR GUESTS LOVE SPREADING SALMON MOUSSE OVER TOASTED BAGELS. IF YOU FIND A TABLESPOON OR SO LEFT OVER, TRY IT INSIDE AN OMELET FOR A VERY RICH AND SATISFYING BREAKFAST SERVED WITH A CHILLED BOWL OF FRESH FRUIT ON THE SIDE. THE MOUSSE WILL KEEP UP TO A WEEK WHEN COVERED AND STORED IN THE REFRIGERATOR.

Chicken pistachio pâté

This pâté needs 2 days to develop its special flavors, and tastes even better if left 2 more days. We serve it on a blanket of greens as a first course, with Quince Chutney (recipe follows) on the side. The pâté's subtle coloring, accented by the brilliance of quince and the vibrancy of fresh greens arranged on a white platter, makes this a special treat to the eye as well as the palate.

4 fresh thyme branches
$^3/_4$ cup finely chopped onion
2 garlic cloves, finely chopped
1 teaspoon grated orange rind
1$^1/_2$ pounds of fresh boneless pork, some fat left on, cut
    into 2-inch chunks
1$^1/_2$ pounds boneless chicken breast, cut into 1$^1/_2$-inch chunks
$^1/_2$ cup Madeira
1 teaspoon Pernod (anise liqueur), or $^1/_2$ teaspoon
    ground aniseed
2 tablespoons salt
2 teaspoons freshly ground black pepper
$^1/_2$ teaspoon dried thyme
$^1/_2$ cup coarsely chopped pistachio nuts

Preheat the oven to 350°F. Butter a 9-by-5-by-3-inch pan.

Arrange the thyme branches across the bottom of the pan.

Place the onion, garlic, and orange rind in the bowl of a food processor. Pulse on and off 5 times. Add the pork and process until it's coarsely chopped. Transfer the mixture to a bowl. Add the rest of the ingredients and, using your hands, knead the mixture until smooth.

Pack the pâté into the loaf pan, pressing hard to force out all the air bubbles. Cover the pan tightly with foil. Set the loaf pan inside a larger roasting pan. Add hot water to the larger pan until it reaches halfway up the sides of the loaf pan. Bake for 1³/₄ hours. Prick the loaf with a thin knife. It is done when the juices run clear.

Remove the loaf pan from the oven and lay 1 or 2 bricks on top of the foil-covered pâté to weigh it down. Let it cool to room temperature, then refrigerate until firm, at least 2 days to develop its flavor. Remove the bricks from the foil. Keep the pâté refrigerated until 1 hour prior to serving.

To serve, invert the pan onto a serving platter so that the thyme branches are on top. Surround the pâté with toasted rounds of bread.

YIELDS 10 SERVINGS AS A FIRST COURSE,
AND MANY WHEN SERVED AS HORS D'OEUVRE

COVERED AND REFRIGERATED,
THE PÂTÉ WILL KEEP
UP TO 7 DAYS.

(continued)

Quince chutney

When cooked, quince turns a deep rose color and holds its shape nicely, making it a lovely garnish for almost any poultry dish. It can be prepared ahead of time and kept up to 4 weeks, covered and stored in the refrigerator.

> *4 large quince, peeled, cored, and cut into chunks*
> *(about 6 cups)*
> *2 lemons, halved and thinly sliced*
> *5 cups finely chopped onions*
> *2 cups red wine vinegar*
> *1 teaspoon salt*
> *3 cups sugar*

Place all the ingredients in a large heavy saucepan and bring to a boil. Lower the heat, cover, and cook for 30 minutes. Uncover, turn up the heat, and, stirring often, cook at a rolling boil for 30 minutes, until some liquid evaporates and the mixture becomes the consistency of chutney. Serve at room temperature.

YIELDS 1^1/$_2$ QUARTS

Mock hare pâté

This rich, finely textured pâté originated in Berlin and is still very popular all over northern Europe. Serve the pâté hot on a bed of dressed greens as a first course. Or serve it cold as a wonderful hors d'oeuvre with cornichons, mustard, and toast on the side. Leftovers make the most delicious sandwiches.

5 inches French bread, sliced
1 cup hot milk
2 tablespoons olive oil
1 cup finely chopped onions
$^3/_4$ pound ground veal
$^3/_4$ pound ground beef
$^3/_4$ pound ground pork
1 tablespoon plus 1 teaspoon salt
$1^1/_2$ teaspoons freshly ground black pepper
1 teaspoon dried fennel seeds
$^1/_2$ teaspoon ground cardamom
2 tablespoons drained and chopped capers
2 eggs
$^3/_4$ cup coarsely chopped bacon

Preheat the oven to 450°F.

Place the bread in a bowl with the hot milk. Press down to soak the bread well. Set aside.

In a skillet, sauté the olive oil and onions over a medium heat until light brown. Set aside.

Place the ground veal, beef, and pork in a large bowl. Add the sautéed onions, salt, pepper, fennel seeds, cardamom, capers, and eggs. Press out some of the milk from the bread and add the bread to the bowl with the ground meats. Knead and mix well to blend all.

(continued)

Scatter the bacon over the bottom of a roasting pan. Shape the meat mixture into a loaf and place it on top of the bacon. Bake for 15 minutes. Lower the oven heat to 350° and bake for 1 hour longer. Remove the pâté from the oven. The juices should run clear when pricked with a fork. Let it stand for 10 minutes to settle its juices before slicing.

If you want to serve the pâté cold, cool it to room temperature, then store it in the refrigerator, covered in plastic wrap, for up to 4 days.

YIELDS 6 SERVINGS AS A FIRST COURSE;
MORE AS AN HORS D'OEUVRE

Roast peppers, onion, and caper spread

A savory spread that we serve on toasted bread rounds or spooned onto crisp endive leaves.

2 very large onions, peeled and sliced ¼ inch thick
2 large red bell peppers, seeded and cut into quarters
¼ cup olive oil
1 teaspoon kosher salt
1 tablespoon capers with their brine

Preheat the oven to 400°F.

Place the onions and peppers on a large baking sheet. Drizzle with the oil and sprinkle with salt. Roast for 35 to 40 minutes, or until the vegetables are soft.

Transfer the mixture and any oil and brown bits to the bowl of a food processor. Process until smooth. Fold in the capers and brine. Transfer to a bowl, cover, and refrigerate until ready to serve.

YIELDS 1½ CUPS

Swedish meatballs with capers and dill

Unthinkable not to have these as part of a holiday buffet or an old-fashioned smorgasbord.

THE MEATBALLS

$1^1/_2$ cups cubed white bread
$^1/_2$ cup hot chicken stock (page 84)
2 tablespoons butter
1 cup finely chopped onions
1 pound lean ground beef
1 egg
1 teaspoon Dijon mustard
$^1/_2$ teaspoon ground cardamom
$^1/_8$ teaspoon ground allspice
1 teaspoon salt
$^1/_2$ teaspoon freshly ground black pepper
1 tablespoon safflower oil

THE SAUCE

3 tablespoons butter
3 tablespoons minced shallots
2 tablespoons flour
$1^1/_2$ cups chicken stock
$^1/_4$ teaspoon salt
$^1/_8$ teaspoon freshly ground black pepper
1 tablespoon drained capers
2 tablespoons chopped fresh dill or flat-leaf parsley

Preheat the oven to 400°F.

To make the meatballs, place the bread cubes in a bowl and pour the chicken stock over them. Press down on the bread to soak it thoroughly. Set aside.

In a small skillet, heat 1 tablespoon of the butter and sauté the onions over low heat for about 8 minutes, until the onions turn glossy. Set aside.

In a large bowl, combine the ground beef with the soaked bread cubes, the sautéed onion, egg, Dijon mustard, cardamom, allspice, salt, and pepper. Knead vigorously until well blended. Shape into two dozen 1¼-inch balls.

In a skillet over high heat, melt the remaining 1 tablespoon butter and the safflower oil. Add half the meatballs. Brown them quickly on both sides. Transfer the cooked meatballs to a baking sheet. Repeat with the remaining meatballs. Transfer the baking sheet to the oven and bake for 15 minutes.

To make the sauce, in a heavy saucepan, melt the butter. Add the shallots and sauté over medium heat for a few minutes. Add the flour and, stirring continuously, cook for 2 minutes. Add the chicken stock. Stirring, bring the sauce to a boil. Cook for 2 minutes at a boil, then add the salt and pepper and stir well.

To serve, transfer the meatballs to a large heated bowl. Ladle the sauce over the meatballs and sprinkle with the capers and dill. Position the bowl on your buffet table and let guests serve themselves.

YIELDS 6 SERVINGS

IF SERVING WITH COCKTAILS,
OMIT THE SAUCE AND SERVE
THE MEATBALLS IN A PRETTY
SERVING BOWL WITH WOODEN
PICKS FOR SPEARING, AND
LOTS OF NAPKINS.

Sausage-filled mushrooms

I love these savory morsels. They are simple to make and are always a great hit at our parties.

> 2 tablespoons olive oil
> 1 cup finely chopped shallots
> 12 ounces mushrooms
> 18 mushroom caps, stems removed and saved for the filling
> 12 ounces sausage meat
> $1/2$ teaspoon red pepper flakes
> $1/2$ teaspoon ground aniseed
> $1/2$ teaspoon salt
> $1/2$ teaspoon fresh thyme, or $1/4$ teaspoon dried
> 4 ounces cream cheese, cut into $1/2$-inch chunks

Preheat the oven to 400°F. 20 minutes before baking time.

In a heavy 9-inch skillet over medium heat, heat the olive oil and sauté the shallots for 5 minutes.

Meanwhile, place the 12 ounces mushrooms and the stems saved from the caps in the bowl of a food processor. Pulse on and off for 5 seconds. Add the chopped mushrooms to the hot skillet. Crumble the sausage meat with your hands and add it to the skillet along with the pepper flakes, aniseed, salt, and thyme. Turn up the heat for about 3 minutes, then lower it to medium. Cook the mixture for 20 minutes. Remove the skillet from the heat and stir in the cream cheese until it's melted.

Spoon the sausage mixture into the mushroom caps and place them on a baking sheet. Bake for 12 to 15 minutes. Serve on a bed of fresh arugula drizzled with balsamic vinaigrette dressing (page 321).

Yields 4 to 6 servings
as a first course

....

If you want to use the
Sausage-Filled
Mushrooms as finger
food, choose smaller
mushroom caps, about
30 of them, and proceed
as above. They can be
served warm or at room
temperature.

....

Shrimp in sesame dressing

Deliciously spicy and great as a first course, hors d'oeuvre, or even as a light lunch accompanied with a salad of winter greens.

> *1 tablespoon peanut oil*
> *1¹/₂ pounds peeled raw shrimp (about 30 medium)*
> *1 tablespoon minced fresh ginger*
> *1 garlic clove, minced*
> *6 scallions, trimmed and finely chopped*

> SESAME DRESSING
>
> *1 garlic clove, finely chopped*
> *1 tablespoon sherry vinegar*
> *1 teaspoon Dijon mustard*
> *1 egg yolk*
> *1 tablespoon soy sauce*
> *1¹/₂ tablespoons toasted sesame oil*
> *³/₄ cup safflower oil*
> *2 tablespoons water*
> *2 bunches arugula, washed and dried*

In a large sauté pan, heat the peanut oil until almost smoking. Add the shrimp and sauté for 2 minutes. Add the ginger, garlic, and scallions. Stir once, turning all the shrimp onto the uncooked side. Sauté for 1 minute longer, then quickly transfer to a chilled bowl to stop the shrimp from cooking any more.

For the dressing, place the garlic, vinegar, mustard, egg yolk, soy sauce, and sesame oil in the bowl of a food processor. Process for 5 seconds. With the motor running, add the safflower oil in a slow stream. When the dressing has thickened, turn off the motor and add the water. Process for 2 seconds. Pour half the dressing over the shrimp, saving the remainder for another use. Toss to blend.

Line 6 plates with dressed arugula leaves (see page 238) and divide the shrimp equally among them.

⁓

YIELDS 6 SERVINGS,
$1^1/_4$ CUPS OF DRESSING

....

COVER AND REFRIGERATE THE
REMAINING SAUCE. IT'S GREAT
OVER CHICKEN SALAD,
INSTEAD OF MAYONNAISE.

....

Curried scallops

Bite-size and gently spicy, serve these on toothpicks at cocktail time, or as a first course on dressed spinach leaves or other salad greens.

$^1/_2$ *cup flour*
3 tablespoons curry powder
$^1/_2$ *teaspoon turmeric*
$^3/_4$ *teaspoon salt*
1 pound whole bay scallops (or sea scallops
     cut in half)
$^1/_2$ *cup peanut oil*

In a large deep plate, combine the flour, curry powder, turmeric, and salt. Coat the scallops with the mixture.

In a large skillet, heat the peanut oil until smoking hot. In batches, sauté the scallops on all sides over high heat for about 2 minutes. Don't crowd the pan. Transfer the scallops to a sheet pan lined with paper towels to drain. Serve warm.

YIELDS 6 SERVINGS

DRESSING FOR SALAD GREENS

MIX TOGETHER 2 TABLESPOONS SHERRY VINEGAR AND 5 TABLESPOONS OLIVE OIL AND DRIZZLE OVER THE GREENS. TOSS TO BLEND.

Tapenade
and sun-dried tomatoes

Ripe olives, sun-dried tomatoes, anchovies, combined with a touch of Cognac! Always a huge success at cocktail parties. For an added treat, try topping the tapenade with small pieces of ripe, creamy goat cheese.

1 cup drained pitted ripe olives in oil
2 garlic cloves, minced
2 anchovy fillets, drained
$1/4$ cup finely chopped sun-dried tomatoes
$1/2$ teaspoon mustard
1 teaspoon fresh lemon juice
2 teaspoons Cognac
2 tablespoons olive oil
$1/2$ teaspoon freshly ground black pepper
4 slices white country-style bread, toasted and cut
    into quarters
3 eggs, hard-boiled

Combine all the ingredients except for the bread and eggs in the bowl of a food processor. Pulse until finely chopped. Store in the refrigerator for use as needed.

To serve as a finger food, spread the tapenade on the toasted bread triangles. Peel and chop the eggs and spoon some onto the tapenade. Serve at room temperature.

YIELDS 16 TAPENADE TRIANGLES

Brandade of smoked trout in potato shells

A wonderfully creamy blending of smoked fish and potatoes with a hint of garlic that seems to bond their individual flavors. As a first course, serve 4 brandade-filled potato shells per person, with lemon wedges on the side. Or arrange the shells on a large platter and serve as an ideal finger food before dinner.

> 24 small potatoes, Yukon Gold or Red Bliss
> 1 baking potato, cut into 6 pieces
> 2 tablespoons plus $^1/_3$ cup olive oil
> 2 smoked trout, bones and skin removed (1$^1/_4$ cups meat)
> 2 garlic cloves, minced
> $^1/_3$ cup heavy cream
> 2 teaspoons fresh lemon juice
> $^1/_2$ teaspoon freshly ground black pepper
> Salt, if needed

Preheat the oven to 350°F.

Place the small potatoes and the cut-up potato in a roasting pan. Drizzle with 2 tablespoons of the olive oil and bake for 40 to 45 minutes, or until they're cooked through.

After the potatoes have cooled, cut a thin slice from the top of each small potato and scoop out most of the pulp. Set the potato shells aside.

Place the pulp in the bowl of a food processor fitted with a metal blade. Remove and discard the skin from the baking potato. Add its pulp to the bowl. Add the smoked trout, garlic, and cream. Process until smooth. Add the remaining $^1/_3$ cup of olive oil, the lemon juice, pepper, and salt if needed. Process until creamy smooth. Spoon the brandade into potatoes shells, mounding the tops.

If you've prepared the dish earlier and have it sitting in the refrigerator, heat the stuffed potatoes uncovered in a 350°F. oven for 15 minutes before serving.

YIELDS 6 SERVINGS AS A FIRST COURSE,
OR 24 HORS D'OEUVRE

Hearty soups
for fall and winter

· ·

*Of all the items on the menu, soup is that which exacts
the most delicate perfection and the strictest attention.*

ESCOFFIER

The recipes we've assembled for winter soups are very different from those
for spring and summer. Again keeping seasonal produce in mind, our winter soups
are heartier and, even though they can be served as ideal first courses, they could
equally be offered as a substantial lunch or a light supper. A steaming bowl of robust soup, a crusty loaf of bread, and a salad tossed in a tangy dressing are, at
times, everything a person could wish for. And these soups can brighten even the
most bitter of winter days. Therefore, many of the recipes were designed to accommodate a large gathering, or larger portions.

We sell batches of soup in early January, just before we close the doors to

Loaves and Fishes, largely because most of them can be frozen. However, I don't recommend freezing any soup that contains dairy products, since it would tend to crystallize and, no matter how much you try, the soup will never reconstitute properly.

Distinct, luscious, and wholesome, these soups will offer you a gratifying assortment of choices throughout the winter months.

Who would not give all else for two
pennyworth only of beautiful soup?

LEWIS CARROLL

Shrimp and swordfish soup

Every February we have a group of 12 businessmen who arrive for their annual meeting. We start the meal with this fish soup, followed by Hazelnut-Crusted Chicken with Mustard Sauce. For dessert we serve a pineapple mousse, rich chocolate bars, and warm chocolate sauce, which bind them deliciously together. The same meal is requested each year.

$^1/_4$ *cup olive oil*

2 cups finely chopped onion

3 cups finely chopped fennel (1 large bulb)

1 cup peeled and chopped carrots

2 tablespoons minced garlic

$^1/_2$ *teaspoon red pepper flakes*

$^1/_2$ *teaspoon crumbled saffron*

1 strip of orange peel, about 5 inches long

$3^1/_2$ *cups clam juice, fresh from your fish store*

4 cups peeled, finely chopped plum tomatoes with their juices

1 pound swordfish, cut into bite-size pieces

1 pound peeled medium shrimp

Salt to taste

2 tablespoons chopped fennel fronds

2 tablespoons chopped fresh parsley

In a large, heavy pot, heat the olive oil, and sauté the onions, fennel, carrots, and garlic over medium heat, about 12 to 15 minutes, until the vegetables are soft and glossy. Add the pepper flakes, saffron, orange peel, clam juice, and tomatoes. Bring to a boil, stirring a few times. Lower the heat and simmer, covered, for 25 minutes. Add the swordfish and shrimp. Continue simmering for another 5 minutes, until the fish is just cooked through. Taste for seasoning. You may want to add a little salt.

Discard the orange peel. Divide the soup among 6 soup plates. Garnish with the fennel fronds and parsley. Serve hot.

Yields 6 servings

You can easily enlarge
this recipe by doubling
all the ingredients.

Ravioli and chicken meatball soup

Made with a clear, rich chicken broth, this soup has become a favorite at Loaves and Fishes. We serve it at the Inn for lunch with our Wild Mushroom Tart and and a crunchy green salad.

$^1/_4$ cup olive oil

4 cups coarsely chopped onions

1 small fennel bulb, julienned

$1^1/_2$ cups peeled and sliced carrots

2 quarts chicken stock (page 84)

$1^1/_4$ teaspoons salt

1 skinless and boneless chicken breast (about 1 pound)

1 tablespoon finely minced shallot

$^1/_4$ cup plain dried bread crumbs

1 egg yolk

$^1/_8$ teaspoon dried thyme

$^1/_4$ teaspoon freshly ground black pepper

3 quarts water

24 cheese- or wild-mushroom-filled ravioli, fresh or frozen

1 tablespoon finely chopped fresh flat-leaf parsley

In a heavy saucepan, heat the olive oil and sauté the onions, fennel, and carrots over low heat for 10 minutes. Make sure the vegetables don't brown. Add the chicken stock and $^3/_4$ teaspoon of the salt and bring to a boil. Lower the heat, cover, and simmer for 25 minutes.

Trim all fat from the chicken breast. Cut the meat into chunks and place in the bowl of a food processor. Pulse 5 times until the chicken is medium-fine. Transfer to a bowl and add the shallots, bread crumbs, egg yolk, dried thyme, the remaining $^1/_2$ teaspoon of salt, and the pepper. With your hands, blend the mixture thoroughly. Shape into 24 balls. Add to the hot soup and simmer for 5 minutes, or until all the meatballs float to the surface.

In a separate pot, bring the water to a rapid boil. Lower the heat and add the ravioli. Simmer for 3 minutes, or until the ravioli float to the top. If using frozen ravioli, cook for 7 to 8 minutes.

Divide the soup among 6 bowls. Add 4 ravioli to each bowl. Sprinkle with the chopped parsley and serve hot.

YIELDS 6 SERVINGS

IF USING FROZEN RAVIOLI,
TRANSFER THEM DIRECTLY
FROM THE FREEZER TO THE
SIMMERING WATER. IF
COOKING FOR A LARGER
GATHERING, YOU CAN DOUBLE
ALL THE INGREDIENTS.

Bean and escarole soup

1¹/₂ cups Great Northern dry white beans
2 tablespoons olive oil
4 cups finely chopped onions
3 cups chopped ham (about ³/₄ pound)
2 garlic cloves, minced
10 cups chicken stock (page 84)
2 fresh bay leaves, or 1 dried
8 sprigs flat-leaf parsley
6 sprigs fresh thyme, or ¹/₂ teaspoon dried
¹/₄ teaspoon freshly ground black pepper
1 head escarole, washed and coarsely chopped
1¹/₂ teaspoons salt
1¹/₂ teaspoons finely chopped fresh parsley

In a pot, cover the beans with water and bring to a boil. Cook for 2 minutes. Remove from the heat and let them stand for 1 hour. Drain and set aside.

In a deep, heavy soup pot, heat the oil and sauté the onions, ham, and garlic over medium heat for 10 minutes, stirring often. Make sure the mixture doesn't brown. Add the beans and chicken stock.

Tie the bay leaf, parsley, and thyme sprigs together with cotton string and add to the pot. If using dried thyme, sprinkle it into the pot. Bring the soup to a boil, lower the heat, cover, and, stirring occasionally, simmer for 2 hours.

Discard the herb bundle. Add the escarole and salt. Stir well. Simmer the soup for 5 minutes, uncovered. Taste and adjust the seasoning.

Serve in deep soup bowls, garnished with the chopped parsley.

Covered and stored in
the refrigerator,
leftovers can be kept
for up to 1 week.

Root vegetable soup

This is a standard recipe we've used over the years with great results; however, almost any combination of root vegetables can be used with the same delicious result.

> 2 tablespoons olive oil
> 2 cups chopped onions
> 2 garlic cloves, minced
> 1 fennel bulb, cut into $1/2$-inch cubes
> 1 medium carrot, peeled, cut into rounds
> 1 medium celeriac, peeled and cubed
> 2 parsnips, peeled, cut into rounds
> 1 bay leaf
> $5^1/2$ cups strong chicken stock (page 84)
> 1 small sweet potato, peeled and cubed
> 1 small baking potato, peeled and cubed
> 1 teaspoon salt
> $1/2$ teaspoon freshly ground black pepper
> $1/4$ cup freshly grated Parmesan cheese
> Fennel fronds, chopped, for garnish

In a large soup pot, heat the olive oil, and sauté the onions, garlic, fennel, carrot, celeriac, and parsnips over medium heat for 10 minutes, stirring often. The vegetables should be glossy, not brown. Add the bay leaf, chicken stock, sweet potato, and white potato, and bring to a boil. Lower the heat, cover, and simmer for 30 minutes, until the vegetables are tender. Season with the salt and pepper.

Serve hot in deep soup plates, sprinkled with Parmesan cheese and chopped fennel fronds.

....

This recipe can easily be doubled to accommodate larger gatherings or appetites.

....

Kale and barley soup

A hearty soup that we serve with a basket of Garlic Bread (see box) on the side.

$^3/_4$ *pound kale, stems removed*
1 cup water
2 tablespoons olive oil
4$^1/_2$ cups finely chopped onions
2 garlic cloves, minced
$^3/_4$ *pound smoked ham, cut into $^1/_2$-inch cubes*
$^3/_4$ *cup dry pearl barley*
10 cups (2$^1/_2$ quarts) chicken stock (page 84)

Place the kale in a large saucepan and add the water. Over medium heat, bring the water to a boil. Lower the heat, cover, and simmer for 5 minutes. Transfer with the liquid to the bowl of a food processor and puree the kale to a fine texture. Set aside.

In a large soup pot, heat the olive oil and sauté the onions and garlic over low heat for 10 minutes, until the onions are soft. Add the ham and barley. Sauté for 5 minutes longer. Add the chicken stock and bring the mixture to a boil. Lower the heat, cover, and, stirring a few times, simmer the soup for 1 hour and 15 minutes. Add the kale and stir well. Cook for 15 minutes. Serve very hot.

YIELDS 6 TO 8 SERVINGS

Garlic Bread

Mash 1 garlic clove into 4 tablespoons softened butter. Spread over both halves of a French loaf split lengthwise. Toast under the broiler until crispy brown.

Pumpkin soup

A deliciously creamy soup for chilly autumn days. Don't throw away the pumpkin seeds. When roasted, they make a superb snack.

> *2 tablespoons butter*
> *2 cups finely chopped onions*
> *1 medium pumpkin, peeled, seeded, and cut into 2-inch cubes ($8^{1}/_{2}$ cups)*
> *$^{3}/_{4}$ cup peeled and chopped potatoes*
> *4 cups chicken stock (page 84)*
> *2 teaspoons salt*
> *$^{1}/_{8}$ teaspoon cayenne*
> *$^{1}/_{4}$ teaspoon grated nutmeg*
> *2 tablespoons heavy cream*

In a large saucepan, melt the butter and sauté the onions over very low heat for 10 minutes, until they are glossy. Add the pumpkin, potatoes, and chicken stock. Bring to a boil. Cook, covered, for 30 minutes. Remove from the heat and cool until safe to handle, about 2 hours.

Transfer the soup in batches to a blender and puree. Pour back into the saucepan. Add the salt, cayenne, nutmeg, and cream. Stirring a few times, reheat the soup just to the boiling point and serve.

YIELDS 4 SERVINGS

ANOTHER SOUP THAT CAN BE
EXPANDED BY DOUBLING ALL
THE INGREDIENTS.

ROASTED PUMPKIN SEEDS

PREHEAT THE OVEN TO 250°F. COAT 2 CUPS WASHED, HULLED, AND DRIED PUMPKIN SEEDS WITH 2 TABLESPOONS SAFFLOWER OIL. SPRINKLE WITH 1 TEASPOON SALT. SPREAD THE SEEDS ON A BAKING SHEET AND ROAST UNTIL THEY'RE CRISP AND BROWN, 45 TO 50 MINUTES.

Main courses
for fall and winter

....

. . . a good dinner and feasting reconciles everybody.

SAMUEL PEPYS

*W*ith the many celebrations surrounding the fall and winter holidays, it is
sometimes difficult to believe that the season will ever end. With our fireplaces
working overtime, all our rooms filled, and with the general bustle and excitement
that comes with this season, we barely notice that the days are beginning to grow
longer. It is only after I have cut some branches of forsythia and popped them into
vases, forcing the blossoms, that I feel a definite change. Our tubs of tulips and daffodils start to bud, and that, too, is a signal that, very soon, all our local farmers
will be on their tractors, creating corduroy rows of newly tilled fields ready for
planting.

Throughout Thanksgiving, Christmas, and New Year's, we feel lucky to be able to plan some really superb dinner parties. Choosing wines has always been as important as shaping the menu. As a general rule when selecting wines, I consider the flavors and textures in the recipe and try to create a harmony between the food and the wine. The fuller and sturdier the food, the more full-bodied the wine. Much has been said about which wine to drink with what foods. Champagne is best served as an aperitif or with dessert. If you ask ten guests what they like best, you will most probably get ten different answers. However, there are a few obvious rules: white before red; light before hearty; young before old. Another added note: Serve only dry *white wines with dinner; sweet wines can dull the taste buds and your guests will not be able to enjoy the dishes you have carefully prepared.*

All the traditional dishes such as Roast Turkey, Goose, and Baked Ham are offered in this section. We have included those because, to me, they represent holiday meals at their finest. I have also included some original recipes that I hope will intrigue you.

I adore the winter months. I enjoy trying to create a home away from home for all our guests. But, as March draws to a close, it gives us a great lift to open the breakfast-room door for the very first time and feel the fresh and mellow breeze that tells us spring is, in fact, just around the corner.

Fill ev'ry glass, for wine inspires us
And fires us
With courage love and joy.

JOHN GAY

Roast lobster with saffron sauce and lima bean puree

Without a doubt, this makes a striking presentation: red lobster nestled on top of a pale green lima bean puree. And the lobster tastes as good as it looks. This is one of our most requested dinners.

10 quarts water
Two 3-pound lobsters
4 tablespoons melted butter

SAFFRON SAUCE

$^1/_3$ cup finely minced shallots
1 tablespoon butter, plus 6 tablespoons ($^3/_4$ stick) cold butter,
    cut into 6 pieces
$^1/_2$ teaspoon crumbled saffron
$1^1/_2$ cups fish stock (page 83) or clam juice
$^1/_3$ cup heavy cream

LIMA BEAN PUREE

$1^1/_2$ pounds ($3^1/_2$ cups) frozen baby lima beans
2 garlic cloves
2 cups fresh parsley leaves, loosely packed
5 tablespoons butter
1 tablespoon sherry vinegar
1 teaspoon salt
$^1/_2$ teaspoon freshly ground black pepper
1 tablespoon finely minced parsley for garnish

(continued)

Preheat the oven to 450°F.

In a large stockpot, bring the water to a boil. Plunge in the lobsters, head first. Cover, bring to a boil again, and cook for 6 minutes. Transfer the lobsters to a cutting board. Discard the water. When the lobsters are cool enough to handle, remove the tails and cut them in half lengthwise. Loosen the meat but do not remove it. Break off the claws. Crack them and remove the meat, in one piece if possible. Brush the lobster tails and claws with the melted butter. Place them in a roasting pan and roast for 8 to 10 minutes, or until the lobster meat is cooked through. Save and freeze the remaining lobster pieces for stock.

To make the sauce, in a saucepan, sauté the shallots and 1 tablespoon of butter for 2 minutes over medium heat. Add the saffron and fish stock and bring to a boil. Lower the heat and simmer for 5 minutes to reduce the liquid to 1 cup. Add the heavy cream. Over low heat, whisk in the cold butter pieces, one piece at a time, until all the butter is incorporated. Remove from the heat and set in a warm place until ready to serve.

To make the lima bean puree, place the lima beans, garlic, and parsley leaves in a saucepan. Cover with water and bring to a boil. Simmer, covered, for 14 minutes. Drain. Transfer the beans to the bowl of a food processor. Add the butter, sherry vinegar, salt, and pepper. Puree until smooth.

To serve, divide the puree among 4 heated dinner plates, spooning it onto the center of each plate. Place a lobster-tail half, in its shell, on top of the puree in each dish. Add 1 lobster claw to each plate for garnish, leaning the claws against the lobster tails. Spoon the sauce around the lobsters. Sprinkle with parsley and serve.

YIELDS 4 SERVINGS

....

WINE SUGGESTION

A DISH AS SPECIAL AS THIS DESERVES
AN EQUALLY SPECIAL WINE. I WOULD
SERVE A GREAT WHITE BURGUNDY
FROM THE CÔTE DE BEAUNE.

....

Vegetable potpie

This is for our vegetarian customers, guests, and friends.

THE PASTRY TOPPING

2 cups flour, chilled
12 tablespoons (1¹/₂ sticks) butter, cold, cut into
*   filbert-size pieces*
¹/₂ teaspoon salt
¹/₄ teaspoon freshly ground black pepper
¹/₂ cup ice cold water

THE FILLING

3 cups 1-inch cubed celeriac
2 cups 1-inch cubed carrots
4 cups 1-inch cubed butternut squash
2 cups 1-inch cubed fennel
1¹/₂ cups 1-inch cubed onions
¹/₃ cup olive oil
1 teaspoon salt

THE SAUCE

6 tablespoons (³/₄ stick) butter
2 garlic cloves, minced
5 tablespoons flour
2¹/₂ cups chicken stock (page 84) (or water, if you are
*   preparing a completely vegetarian meal)*
¹/₄ cup crème fraîche
¹/₂ teaspoon salt
¹/₄ teaspoon freshly ground black pepper

(continued)

3 tablespoons finely chopped fennel fronds
¼ cup finely chopped fresh flat-leaf parsley

EGG WASH

1 egg yolk
1 tablespoon heavy cream

For the pastry, combine the flour, butter, salt, and pepper in the bowl of a food processor. Pulse 4 times. Add the water. Process until the pastry is still crumbly but starts to stick together. Transfer the dough to a floured surface. With your hands, knead the mixture until it just holds together. Chill in the refrigerator for 30 minutes or longer.

Preheat the oven to 400°F.

For the filling, place the chopped vegetables, olive oil, and salt in a bowl. Toss to combine. Transfer to a baking sheet large enough to hold all the vegetables in one layer and roast them for 40 minutes, or until they're tender. Reduce the oven heat to 375°.

To make the sauce, melt the butter in a heavy saucepan. Add the garlic and flour and cook for 1 minute, stirring constantly, until smooth. Remove from the heat and add all the chicken stock at once. Stir and return to medium heat. Still stirring, bring the mixture to a boil. Stir for 2 minutes. Continuing to stir, add the crème fraîche, salt, and pepper. Bring the sauce to a boil again. Lower the heat and simmer for 1 minute longer. Remove from the heat. Add the roasted vegetables, fennel fronds, and parsley and mix well. Divide the mixture into four 16-ounce ovenproof bowls or one 2-quart casserole.

On a floured surface, roll out the chilled dough into a large rectangle, ¼ inch thick. Cut the pastry into 4 rounds, slightly larger than the bowls. Lay the pastry on top of the filling, with the dough overlapping the edges of the bowls. Press the dough along the edges to seal. Cut a couple of slits in the top to allow the steam to escape.

If using a casserole, cover it with the pastry rectangle. Trim the edges to a ¾-inch overlap. Press the dough to seal, and cut a couple of slits in the top.

In a small bowl, whisk together the egg yolk and cream and brush the wash over the top of the pastry. Set the bowls on a baking sheet. Bake for 45 minutes, or until the mixture is bubbling and the pastry has browned nicely.

To turn this into a
seafood potpie, tuck 3 or 4
raw shrimp and scallops
into each prepared potpie
bowl. Cover with the
crust and bake as
directed.

WINE SUGGESTIONS

This homey, wintry
dish would be
equally good with
a light Côte du
Rhône or a
medium-bodied
Pouilly-Fumé.

Tuna burgers with coriander-lime mayonnaise

Easy to prepare and delicious to have on those evenings when all you want is a light meal.

2 tablespoons olive oil

2 cups finely diced onions

2 pounds fresh tuna, dark meat and skin removed

3 tablespoons heavy cream

1$^1/_2$ cups homemade bread crumbs (page 108)

$^1/_2$ cup finely diced red bell pepper

$^1/_2$ cup finely diced celery

4 scallions, trimmed and finely chopped

2 tablespoons finely chopped fresh coriander leaves

1 tablespoon drained capers

1 egg plus 1 egg white

1 tablespoon salt

1 teaspoon freshly ground black pepper

$^1/_3$ cup peanut oil

CORIANDER-LIME MAYONNAISE

2 egg yolks

3 tablespoons fresh lime juice

1 teaspoon soy sauce

$^1/_2$ teaspoon toasted sesame oil

$^3/_4$ teaspoon mustard

$^1/_4$ teaspoon Tabasco sauce

1 teaspoon minced fresh garlic

1 cup fresh coriander leaves, loosely packed

1¹/₄ cups peanut oil
¹/₂ teaspoon salt

Preheat the oven to 425°F.

In a skillet, heat the olive oil and sauté the onions for 8 minutes over medium heat, until they are light brown. Set aside.

Cut half the tuna into chunks and place it in the bowl of a food processor. Add the cream and process to a fine puree. Transfer the tuna to a large bowl. Add the sautéed onions. Dice the remaining tuna into ¹/₄-by-¹/₄-inch pieces and add to the bowl. Add the rest of the ingredients, except the peanut oil, and knead the tuna mixture into a firm ball. Shape into 6 burgers.

Heat the peanut oil in a large skillet. Without crowding the pan, place the burgers in the hot oil. Sauté both sides over high heat, until the burgers are a medium brown. Transfer the tuna burgers to a sheet pan and bake for 12 minutes or until done to your taste.

To make the coriander-lime mayonnaise, place the egg yolks, lime juice, soy sauce, sesame oil, and mustard in the bowl of a food processor fitted with the metal blade. Pulse 3 times. Add the Tabasco sauce, garlic, and coriander leaves and pulse 10 times. With the motor running, add the peanut oil through the feed tube. First in droplets, then, as the mayonnaise starts to thicken, in a slow, steady stream. Add the salt and stir. Transfer the mayonnaise to a small sauceboat to serve with the tuna burgers.

YIELDS 6 SERVINGS, 1¹/₄ CUPS MAYONNAISE

....

WINE SUGGESTIONS

TRY A RICH AROMATIC
GEWÜRZTRAMINER
FROM ALSACE, OR A
LIGHT RED, SUCH AS A
BEAUJOLAIS.

....

Fish and chips

Our version of a perennial favorite enjoyed by children and adults alike. Offer some ketchup on the side or, as they do in England, malt vinegar.

THE CHIPS

2 pounds baking potatoes
$1/4$ cup olive oil
1 teaspoon kosher salt

THE FISH

$1/4$ cup milk
$1^1/3$ cups coarsely ground yellow cornmeal
$1^1/2$ teaspoons salt
1 teaspoon freshly ground black pepper
$1/2$ cup peanut oil
$1^1/2$ pounds flounder fillets
1 tablespoon chopped fresh parsley
1 lemon, cut into wedges

Preheat the oven to 425°F.

To make the chips, cut the potatoes into $1/3$-by-$1/3$-by-2-inch sticks. Place them in a bowl and toss with the olive oil and salt. Coat them well, then transfer them to a sheet pan and bake for 40 minutes, or until they're crispy brown and tender.

For the fish, pour the milk into a shallow plate. In another shallow plate, combine the cornmeal, salt, and pepper.

In a large skillet, heat the peanut oil until smoking hot. Dip the fillets first into the milk, then into the cornmeal, coating both sides evenly. Sauté the fish over high heat for 1 minute on each side or until light brown and cooked through. Do this in several batches to ensure that the fillets do not touch.

Transfer the sautéed fish to a large platter. Sprinkle with chopped parsley and garnish with lemon wedges. Serve hot, with the chips on the side.

YIELDS 4 SERVINGS

WINE SUGGESTION

I LIKE A CRISP SANCERRE, WELL CHILLED, WITH THIS SIMPLE MEAL. SOME MAY PREFER TO DRINK BEER WITH THIS DISH.

Hazelnut-coated chicken breasts with mustard sauce

A delectably nutty coating. A mild mustard sauce. Perfect.

> 2 pounds skinless and boneless chicken breasts, all fat
>   removed, halved
> ¹/₄ cup Dijon mustard
> ³/₄ cup ground hazelnuts
> ¹/₂ cup dried bread crumbs
> 1 teaspoon salt
> 1 teaspoon freshly ground black pepper
> ¹/₄ cup peanut oil

MUSTARD SAUCE

> 2 tablespoons butter
> ¹/₃ cup finely chopped shallots
> ³/₄ cup strong chicken or veal stock (page 84 or 86)
> 3 tablespoons Dijon mustard
> ¹/₂ cup crème fraîche

Preheat the oven to 350°F.

Coat the chicken breasts on all sides with the mustard. On a separate plate, combine the hazelnuts, bread crumbs, salt, and pepper.

In a large skillet, heat the oil until smoking. Dredge the cutlets in the hazelnut-crumb mixture, pressing down on both sides, getting as much of the mixture as possible to adhere to the cutlets. Sauté the cutlets over medium heat, 5 to 6 minutes per side, until they're browned on both sides. Transfer to a roasting pan and bake for 15 minutes.

To make the sauce, wipe the skillet with a paper towel, place the skillet over medium heat, and melt the butter. Add the shallots and, stirring a few times, sauté until they're light brown. Turn the heat high and add the chicken or veal stock. Cook for 30 seconds. Add the mustard and crème fraîche. Whisk to blend. Cook the sauce for 30 seconds longer, or until it starts to thicken. Serve hot, with the chicken cutlets.

YIELDS 4 SERVINGS

WINE SUGGESTIONS

CÔTE RÔTIE, A RED FROM THE NORTHERN RHÔNE VALLEY, WOULD BE MY FIRST CHOICE— OR A GEWÜRZTRAMINER FROM CALIFORNIA. WITH A HINT OF SWEETNESS, BOTH WINES WORK WELL WITH THE CHICKEN AND SAUCE.

Thyme-crusted chicken breasts with sautéed apples and cider sauce

5 tablespoons butter
1 teaspoon sugar
4 tart apples, peeled, cored, cut into wedges
4 chicken cutlets (approximately 2 pounds)
2 teaspoons dried thyme leaves
2 teaspoons salt
2 teaspoons freshly ground black pepper
3 tablespoons peanut oil
$^1/_2$ cup minced shallots
2 tablespoons Calvados (apple brandy)
$^1/_2$ cup apple cider
1 cup heavy cream
Fresh thyme sprigs for garnish

Preheat the oven to 200°F.

In a large skillet, melt 2 tablespoons of the butter. Sprinkle in the sugar. When the skillet is hot, add the apples and sauté for 2 minutes, then transfer the apples to an ovenproof plate. Place in the warm oven until ready to use.

Trim the chicken cutlets of all fat. Season with the thyme, salt, and pepper, pressing it onto both sides of the cutlets.

Add the peanut oil and the remaining 3 tablespoons of butter to the skillet. So as not to crowd the pan, sauté the cutlets in batches over medium heat, 6 minutes per side, until they're cooked through. Transfer the cutlets to a plate and place them in the warm oven.

In the same skillet, sauté the shallots, tossing them for about 2 minutes to make sure they cook on all sides. Add the Calvados and cook for 1 minute longer. Add the apple cider and cream and, stirring constantly, bring the mixture to a boil over high heat until the sauce starts to thicken. This should take about 2 minutes.

To serve, place a chicken cutlet on each of the 4 plates. Nap each with some sauce. Place the sautéed apples around the cutlet and garnish with the thyme sprigs. Serve hot.

YIELDS 4 SERVINGS

WINE SUGGESTION

AN IMPORTANT
CALIFORNIA
CHARDONNAY FROM
THE SONOMA AREA
WOULD BE A PERFECT
MATCH.

Crispy-skinned roast duck

The ginger, honey, and orange juice turns the duck skin brown and crispy and gives the meat just the right amount of zest.

> *One 5-pound duck*
> *1 orange, cut into chunks*
> *2 tablespoons olive oil*
> *2 teaspoons salt*
> *1 teaspoon freshly ground black pepper*
> *1½ cups finely chopped onions*

> ### The sauce
>
> *3 garlic cloves, finely chopped*
> *¼ cup peeled and finely chopped fresh ginger*
> *⅓ cup honey*
> *2 tablespoons fresh lemon juice*
> *1½ cups strong hot tea*
> *¾ cup fresh orange juice*
> *1 teaspoon salt*
> *2 teaspoons arrowroot or cornstarch*
> *2 tablespoons water*

Preheat the oven to 325°F.

Rinse the duck well under cold running water. Pat it dry with paper towels. Remove and discard all excess fat from the cavity and neck area. Stuff the orange chunks into the cavity. Rub the skin with the olive oil, salt, and pepper. Sprinkle the chopped onions into a roasting pan and place the duck, breast side down, on top of them. Roast for 1 hour.

For the sauce, combine the garlic and ginger in the bowl of a food processor and pulse on and off for 1 minute. Add the honey, lemon juice, and hot tea. Pulse for 1 minute. Add the orange juice and salt and pulse for 2 minutes more.

Remove the duck from the oven and turn it breast side up. Pour the prepared sauce over the duck. Increase the oven temperature to 425° and roast the duck for 1 more hour. Remove from oven. The juices should run clear when the inside of the leg is pricked with a fork. Transfer the duck to a large serving platter.

In a small saucepan, combine the arrowroot or cornstarch with the water until smooth. Strain the sauce from the roasting pan into the saucepan. Stirring constantly, bring the sauce to a full boil. Pour into a sauceboat to serve on the side. With poultry shears, cut the duck into 4 pieces, discarding the backbone.

YIELDS 4 SERVINGS

WE USE LONG ISLAND DUCK FOR THIS RECIPE; HOWEVER, ANY DUCK WITH AN AMPLE AMOUNT OF BREAST MEAT WOULD BE SUITABLE FOR ROASTING. IF YOU CANNOT FIND A 5- TO 5$^{1}/_{2}$-POUND DUCK, USE 2 SMALLER ONES.

WINE SUGGESTIONS

THIS ENTRÉE GOES BEST WITH A RED FROM THE SOUTH OF FRANCE, SUCH AS A ST.-EMILION, OR A HAUT-MÉDOC FROM BORDEAUX.

Roast turkey with apple, orange, and raisin stuffing

Thanksgiving is one of our favorite holidays because it centers around family, friends, food, and drink. And what could be a better centerpiece than roast turkey with a sweet and savory stuffing and a smooth rich gravy? We usually serve a sweet and tangy Cranberry-Pear Sauce (see box) on the side.

THE STUFFING

8 cups ³/₄-inch cubed day-old bread
8 tablespoons (1 stick) butter
4 cups finely chopped onions
3 cups finely chopped celery
3 cups coarsely chopped tart apples
1 tablespoon salt
2 teaspoons freshly ground black pepper
¹/₂ teaspoon dried thyme leaves
1 small orange, cut into quarters, pits removed
³/₄ cup raisins
¹/₃ cup finely chopped fresh flat-leaf parsley
2 cups chicken stock (page 84)

THE TURKEY

One 14- to 16-pound fresh turkey
2 tablespoons olive oil
1 tablespoon salt

2 tablespoons butter
Neck and giblets from the turkey
1 large onion, quartered
5 cups plus 3 tablespoons water
6 parsley sprigs
1/2 cup port wine
2 tablespoons arrowroot or cornstarch
Salt and freshly ground pepper, if needed
Lots of fresh thyme and Lady apples for garnish

Preheat the oven to 375°F.

To make the stuffing, place the bread cubes on a sheet pan and toast in the oven for 12 to 15 minutes. Remove from the oven and cool. Set aside. This can be done the day before.

Melt the butter in a large saucepan. Add the onions, celery, and apples. Sauté over medium heat for 10 minutes. Add the salt, pepper, thyme, and toasted bread cubes. Remove from the heat.

Place the orange quarters in the bowl of a food processor and chop until fine. Add to the stuffing mixture. Then add the raisins, parsley, and chicken stock. Stir well. Transfer the stuffing to a large bowl and cool to room temperature.

For the turkey, loosely fill the large cavity of the bird with two thirds of the stuffing. Tie the turkey legs with cotton twine to hold the stuffing in place. Scoop the remainder of the stuffing into the neck cavity. Fold the loose neck skin under the turkey to hold the stuffing in place.

Place the turkey in a large roasting pan. Rub the skin with the olive oil and salt. Roast in the oven for 3 1/2 hours. After the turkey has turned golden brown, cover it with foil to keep it from drying out, and continue roasting until done. To test for doneness, pierce the thigh with a fork, if the juices run clear the turkey is ready.

(continued)

To make the sauce, melt the butter in a large saucepan. Add the neck, giblets, and onion. Brown on all sides. Add the 5 cups of water and parsley sprigs. Bring to a boil, lower the heat, cover, and simmer for 1¹/₂ hours.

Transfer the turkey to a large serving platter.

Place the roasting pan over high heat and strain the giblet stock into the pan. Discard the giblets. Scrape up all the brown bits from the bottom of the roasting pan to enrich the gravy. Stirring, cook for 2 minutes. Strain the sauce into a saucepan. Discard any solids. Add the port wine. Combine the arrowroot or cornstarch with the 3 tablespoons of water and add this mixture to the sauce. Bring to a boil and cook for 2 minutes, stirring continually. Taste for seasoning and add salt and pepper if necessary. Pour the sauce into a sauceboat. Garnish the turkey with thyme branches and Lady apples.

YIELDS 6 TO 8 SERVINGS,
WITH PLENTY OF LEFTOVERS

WINE SUGGESTIONS

THANKSGIVING IS THE
TIME FOR BEAUJOLAIS
NOUVEAU, OR, IF YOU
PREFER A WHITE, A
DRY VOUVRAY WOULD
BE MY CHOICE.

CRANBERRY-PEAR SAUCE

THIS GOES BEAUTIFULLY WITH ANY POULTRY DISH, GRILLED OR ROASTED.

3 cups fresh cranberries
3 cups peeled, cored, and cut-up pears
1¼ cups sugar
½ cup apple juice
1 tablespoon cider vinegar
Grated rind of 1 orange
¼ teaspoon freshly ground black pepper

IN A HEAVY SAUCEPAN, COMBINE ALL THE INGREDIENTS AND BRING TO A BOIL. LOWER THE HEAT, COVER, AND, STIRRING OFTEN, COOK FOR 15 MINUTES. SPOON THE SAUCE INTO A SERVING DISH AND CHILL FOR AT LEAST 3 HOURS.

YIELDS 4 CUPS

Turkey meatloaf

A delicious meatloaf that requires very little effort and can easily be converted into great Turkey Burgers.

> 1 cup chopped onions
> 2 garlic cloves
> 2 pounds turkey meat, cut into 2-inch chunks
> 1 teaspoon ground sage
> 1 tablespoon salt
> 1 teaspoon freshly ground black pepper
> 2 eggs
> $^1/_4$ cup plain dried bread crumbs
> $^1/_4$ cup chicken stock (page 84) or milk

Preheat the oven to 375°F.

Using a food processor, puree the onions and garlic. Add the turkey meat and pulse 5 times, until the meat is coarsely ground. Transfer the mixture to a bowl. Add the rest of the ingredients and, with your hands, knead until everything is well combined. Shape into a loaf and place in a small roasting pan. Bake, uncovered, for 1 hour, or until a meat thermometer registers 160°F. To test for doneness, insert a thin knife into the center of the loaf. The juices should run clear.

SERVES 4 TO 6 WITH LEFTOVERS

WINE SUGGESTIONS

SERVE A LIGHT RED,
SUCH AS PINOT NOIR
FROM THE NAPA
VALLEY; OR A SIMPLE
TAVEL, A ROSÉ FROM
FRANCE.

TURKEY BURGERS

PREHEAT THE OVEN TO 375°F. SHAPE THE TURKEY MIXTURE INTO 10 BURGER-SIZE PATTIES. COAT BOTH SIDES WITH CORNMEAL. ADD 2 TABLESPOONS PEANUT OIL TO A SKILLET AND, OVER HIGH HEAT, SAUTÉ THE PATTIES ON BOTH SIDES UNTIL BROWN. TRANSFER THE PATTIES TO A ROASTING PAN AND BAKE FOR 25 MINUTES. SERVE HOT!

Red wine braised pheasant with baked pears

When fall rolls around, this is one of the dishes I look forward to serving. Pheasant, with its distinctive taste, goes superbly with seasonal pears and browned pearl onions.

> *Two 2^1/$_2$-pound pheasants, rinsed and each one cut*
> *into 4 pieces (remove and reserve the backbones*
> *and wing tips)*
> *1 tablespoon kosher or sea salt*
> *1 teaspoon freshly ground black pepper*
> *2 tablespoons olive oil*
> *4 tablespoons butter*
> *3 cups finely chopped onions*
> *1 cup finely chopped carrots*
> *1 strip of orange peel, about 5 inches long*
> *1 bottle heavy red wine, such as Merlot*
> *1 bay leaf*
> *4 sprigs fresh thyme, or ^{1}/$_2$ teaspoon dried*
> *3 cups sliced cremini mushrooms*
> *2 pears, halved lengthwise and cored*
> *3 cups pearl onions*
> *2 tablespoons sugar*
> *^{1}/$_4$ cup crème fraîche or heavy cream*
> *6 sprigs fresh thyme, for garnish*

Preheat the oven to 375°F.

Rub the pheasant pieces on all sides with salt and pepper. In a sauté pan, heat the olive oil and 2 tablespoons of the butter and sauté the pheasant, in batches, until dark brown on both sides. Transfer the pieces to a roasting pan with a tight-fitting lid. To the same sauté pan, add the chopped onions and carrots. Stirring a few times, sauté the vegetables until nicely browned. Add the orange peel, red wine, bay leaf, thyme, mushrooms, and the pheasant backbones and wing tips. Bring to a boil, scraping up all the brown bits from the bottom of the pan to enhance the flavor. Pour the mixture over the pheasant. Cover and roast for 1 hour 15 minutes.

Melt the remaining 2 tablespoons of butter and pour into an ovenproof glass dish. Add the pears, cut side down, and the pearl onions. Sprinkle with the sugar and roast in the oven with the pheasant for the last 40 minutes of roasting time.

Transfer the pheasant to a serving platter. Discard the backs and wing tips. Keep the pheasant warm in a 200° oven until ready to serve.

Strain the cooking liquid into a saucepan. Discard the solids. Add the crème fraîche or cream and stir well to blend. Bring the sauce to a boil. Pour into a sauceboat and serve on the side.

Garnish the platter with the cut-up pears, pearl onions, and fresh thyme.

YIELDS 4 TO 6 SERVINGS

WINE SUGGESTIONS

TRY A FINE RED
BURGUNDY OR A
CABERNET SAUVIGNON
FROM CALIFORNIA.

Roast goose with fruit and onion stuffing and wine-poached quince

There is nothing quite as wonderful as the crisp skin and dark, flavorful meat of a roast goose. This savory-sweet stuffing, one of my favorites, and the Wine-Poached Quince (recipe follows) are such an added treat. This is what I serve my family at Christmas.

One 10- to 12-pound goose
2 teaspoons salt
1 teaspoon freshly ground black pepper
1 teaspoon ground sage

THE STUFFING

1 tablespoon butter
4 cups finely chopped onions
2 apples, halved, cored, and cut into thin slices
2 pears, peeled, halved, cored, and cut into thin slices
12 pitted prunes, cut in half
1 cup soft bread crumbs
$^{1}/_{2}$ teaspoon dried thyme
$^{1}/_{2}$ teaspoon grated nutmeg
$^{1}/_{2}$ cup chicken stock (page 84)
1 teaspoon salt
$1^{1}/_{2}$ teaspoon freshly ground black pepper

1 cup minced shallots
1¹/₂ cups chicken stock
1 cup Madeira wine
2 teaspoons arrowroot
2 tablespoons water

Preheat the oven to 400°F.

Rub the goose inside and out with salt and pepper. Rub the sage into the cavity.

For the stuffing, in a skillet, melt the butter and sauté the onions over medium heat until they are transparent. Add the apple slices, pear slices, and prunes. Sauté over low heat for 15 minutes, or until the fruits become soft. Remove from the heat. Add the remaining stuffing ingredients and mix well. Stuff the mixture into the cavity of the goose. Loosely tie the legs together with cotton string. Tuck the wings under the bird and set the goose in a roasting pan. Add 1 inch of boiling water to the pan. Roast the goose for 1 hour.

Remove from the oven, pour off and discard the water and fat. Return the goose to the oven and roast for 1¹/₂ hours longer. Transfer the goose to a large ovenproof platter. Lowering the oven heat to 200°, place the goose in the warm oven until ready to serve.

To make the sauce, place the shallots in the roasting pan, and sauté over medium heat for a few minutes, just to soften them. Add the chicken stock and Madeira. Stir well, scraping up all the brown bits that add richness to the sauce. Bring to a full boil, then remove from the heat and strain the sauce into a saucepan.

Dissolve the arrowroot in the water, then pour the mixture into the sauce. Stirring constantly, bring the sauce to a boil.

Present the roast goose at the table with the sauce on the side.

YIELDS 5 TO 6 SERVINGS

(continued)

WINE SUGGESTIONS

A CABERNET SAUVIGNON,
A PINOT NOIR, OR A
SYRAH, ALL FROM
CALIFORNIA VINEYARDS,
GOES WELL. I HAVE
SERVED ALL OF THEM AT
ONE TIME OR ANOTHER
AND FIND THEM ALL
EXCELLENT WITH DARK-
MEAT POULTRY.

Wine-poached quince

Absolutely wonderful as an accompaniment to chicken, duck, goose, or pork roasts. Allow 2 quince halves per person, warming the quince in the oven for a few minutes.

> *2 cups dry red wine*
> *1 cup water*
> *1 cup sugar*
> *1 cinnamon stick*
> *2 whole cloves*
> *6 quince, peeled, halved, and cored*

In a saucepan, combine the wine, water, sugar, cinnamon stick, and cloves and bring to a boil. Add the prepared quince halves. Bring to a boil once more, then lower the heat and simmer for 20 minutes, or until the quince is cooked through. This will depend on its ripeness. Refrigerate the quince in its liquid until ready to serve.

YIELDS 6 SERVINGS

Rabbit braised in wine, onions, mushrooms, and herbs

Marinating rabbit in vinegar and herbs not only tenderizes the meat but also helps restore its natural wild taste. Because of the marinating time, this is a dish that should be prepared the day before your gathering.

The marinade

1 cup red wine vinegar
5 juniper berries, crushed
3 garlic cloves, mashed
³/₄ cup thinly sliced onion
¹/₂ teaspoon dried thyme
¹/₂ teaspoon dried rosemary
1 bay leaf
¹/₂ teaspoon freshly ground black pepper

One 3- to 3¹/₂-pound rabbit, cut into 6 pieces
¹/₃ pound sliced smoked bacon, cut into 2-inch pieces
¹/₄ cup olive oil
2 teaspoons salt
³/₄ teaspoon freshly ground black pepper
2 cups finely chopped onions
2 garlic cloves, minced
2 cups coarsely chopped Portobello mushrooms
3 cups red wine
1 cup chicken stock (page 84)
1 large sprig fresh rosemary
2 bay leaves

(continued)

5 sprigs curly parsley
4 plum tomatoes, coarsely chopped
1 tablespoon arrowroot
1/2 cup heavy cream
2 tablespoons chopped fresh parsley, for garnish

In a bowl, combine all the marinade ingredients. Place the rabbit pieces in an earthenware or glass dish and pour the marinade over the meat. Cover the dish and refrigerate for at least 12 or up to 48 hours.

Preheat the oven to 375°F.

In a large, heavy skillet, sauté the bacon until crisp, then transfer it to a medium-size roasting pan. Add the olive oil to the skillet. Dry the rabbit pieces with paper towels, rub the skin with the salt and pepper, and place the rabbit in the skillet. Cook, turning the pieces in the hot fat until both sides are a deep dark brown. Transfer the pieces to the roasting pan. To the skillet, add the onions, garlic, and mushrooms. Sauté over high heat until brown. Add the wine, chicken stock, rosemary, and bay leaves. Cook for 2 minutes. Pour the sauce over the rabbit pieces in the roasting pan. In the same skillet, cook down the marinade to 1/2 cup. Pour this over the rabbit. Place the parsley sprigs and tomatoes in the roasting pan. Cover with foil and roast for 1 1/2 hours.

Transfer the rabbit to a serving platter. Strain the pan juices into a saucepan, reserving the solids. Bring the sauce to a boil. Taste for seasoning. Combine the arrowroot and cream. Add this mixture to the sauce, stirring constantly until it thickens. Pour some of the sauce over the rabbit and serve the rest on the side. Spoon the strained vegetables around the rabbit. Sprinkle with the chopped parsley and serve hot.

YIELD 4 TO 6 SERVINGS

WINE SUGGESTION

A CABERNET FROM THE
NAPA VALLEY IS EXCELLENT
WITH THIS DISH.

Osso buco

Here's our version of the immensely popular Italian classic, which we serve with a steaming mound of rice.

1/3 cup finely chopped pancetta

3 tablespoons olive oil

1/4 cup flour

2 teaspoons salt

1/2 teaspoon freshly ground black pepper

Six 2-inch-thick veal shanks

4 cups finely chopped onions

4 garlic cloves, minced

1 cup finely chopped carrots

4 cups sliced cremini mushrooms

1 1/2 cups dry white wine

1 1/2 cups chicken stock (page 84)

2 cups canned peeled Italian tomatoes with their juices

2 tablespoons finely chopped fresh parsley

Preheat the oven to 350°F.

In a stovetop-to-oven pan, sauté the pancetta over medium heat for 3 to 4 minutes until brown. Remove it to a large plate with a slotted spoon. Add the olive oil to the same pan. Coat the veal shanks evenly with a mixture of flour, salt, and pepper. Brown the shanks in the hot oil for 8 to 10 minutes until they're nicely browned on both sides. Place the shanks on the plate with the pancetta.

(continued)

To the same sauté pan, add the onions, garlic, carrots, and mushrooms and sauté over medium heat, stirring a few times, until brown. Place the veal and pancetta on top of the vegetables. Pour in the wine, chicken stock, and tomatoes. Bring to a boil, cover the pan tightly with a lid or foil, and transfer to the oven to bake for 2 hours.

To serve, place 1 shank on each of 6 heated plates. Spoon some of the sauce over the meat, and garnish with the chopped parsley.

YIELDS 6 SERVINGS

WINE SUGGESTION

A CALIFORNIA MERLOT IS AN EXCELLENT CHOICE FOR THIS HEARTY DISH.

Roast rack of pork with a sage-spice rub on a bed of apple-onion marmalade

Finally, this tender, lean white meat has become suitable dinner party fare. Here is a knockout dinner that is requested time and again. I have my butcher crack and French the bones, which makes life easier and provides a beautiful presentation at the dinner table.

APPLE-ONION MARMALADE

1/4 cup olive oil

3 cups thinly sliced onions

1 teaspoon salt

1 teaspoon freshly ground black pepper

4 apples, halved, cored, and sliced

THE ROAST

1 tablespoon salt

2 garlic cloves

1 tablespoon ground sage

1/2 teaspoon cayenne

2 teaspoons dried thyme

1/4 cup Dijon mustard

One 4- to 4 1/2-pound rack of pork, trimmed of fat,
    bones Frenched

2 tablespoons olive oil

2 cups coarsely chopped onions

1 bunch fresh sage for garnish

(continued)

THE SAUCE

2 cups strong veal stock (page 86)
¹/₄ cup dry port wine
¹/₄ cup heavy cream
1 tablespoon arrowroot dissolved in 1 tablespoon of water

Preheat the oven to 425°F.

To make the marmalade, brush the bottom of a large roasting pan with the olive oil. Add the onions, spread in one layer. Sprinkle with the salt and pepper. Roast for 15 minutes. Place the apples on top of the onions. Don't stir. Roast for 45 minutes longer. Remove from the oven and set aside.

For the pork, mash the salt and garlic into a paste. Rub the sage, cayenne, thyme, and mustard into the paste and brush it over both sides of the meat.

Spread the olive oil over the bottom of a second roasting pan. Add the chopped onions, scattering them over the bottom, and set the roast on top. Roast for 1 hour 15 minutes, or until a meat thermometer inserted in the center of the pork registers 150°.

Transfer the meat to a serving platter. Surround the roast with the onion-apple marmalade. Keep it warm in a 200° oven until ready to serve.

To make the sauce, pour the veal stock into the roasting pan set over medium heat. Bring to a boil, scraping up all the brown bits to enrich the sauce. Strain the liquid into a small saucepan. Add the port wine, cream, and dissolved arrowroot. Stirring constantly, bring to a boil. When slightly thickened, remove from the heat and pour into a sauceboat. Serve hot.

Garnish the roast with fresh sage and serve with the sauce on the side.

YIELDS 6 SERVINGS

....

WINE SUGGESTIONS

IF YOU CAN FIND A RED BAIRRADA
GARRAFEIRA FROM PORTUGAL, BY
ALL MEANS SERVE IT—OR A DRY
SPANISH ROSÉ.

....

COUNTRY WEEKEND ENTERTAINING

Roast boneless pork loin with prunes and wine sauce

This traditional, robust European dish is a truly marvelous meal. The prunes and wine sauce can be prepared first and reheated just before serving.

THE SAUCE

6 ounces pitted prunes
1/2 cup water
2 tablespoons olive oil
3/4 cup finely chopped carrots
1 cup finely chopped shallots
2 tablespoons red wine vinegar
1 1/2 cups red wine
2 tablespoons cold butter
One 2 1/2- to 3-pound boneless pork loin, trimmed of all fat
2 tablespoons olive oil
2 teaspoons fresh thyme leaves, or 1 teaspoon dried
1 teaspoon salt
2 teaspoons freshly ground black pepper

Preheat the oven to 400°F.

For the sauce, place the prunes and water in a saucepan, cover, and cook for 10 minutes. Set aside.

In a skillet, heat the olive oil and sauté the carrots and shallots over medium heat until brown. Add the vinegar and red wine. Cover and simmer over very low heat for 20 minutes. Strain the liquid into the saucepan holding the prunes. Discard the solids. Over medium heat, swirl the butter into the red wine sauce until it's melted. Remove from the heat and set aside.

(continued)

Place the pork in a roasting pan. Combine the olive oil, thyme, salt, and pepper in a small bowl. Rub the mixture into and around the pork loin. Roast the meat for 1 hour, or until a meat thermometer reads 150°.

Remove the roast from the oven and let it rest for 5 minutes to settle its juices. Reheat the wine sauce. Spoon some sauce and 3 prunes onto each of 4 plates. Place 2 slices of pork roast on top, and garnish with any vegetables you have prepared.

YIELDS 4 SERVINGS

WINE SUGGESTIONS

SERVE A RED CHIANTI
FROM ITALY OR, FOR
SOMETHING SPECIAL, A
PESQUERA RESERVA
FROM SPAIN.

Baked ham with mustard and orange glaze

Ham always seems to stretch so well; that's why it is such a perfect addition to any holiday buffet. Leftovers are great the next morning with scrambled eggs, stuffed in sandwiches for lunch, or as a satisfying late-night snack. We like to serve the ham with freshly baked Corn Bread (recipe follows) and store-bought Swedish lingonberries on the side.

> One 10- to 12-pound fully cooked ham, with bone
> 4 cups apple cider
> $1\frac{1}{2}$ cups orange marmalade
> 1 cup Dijon mustard
> 1 cup dark brown sugar, packed
> 1 bunch kale, for garnish

Preheat the oven to 350°F.

Trim away the skin and most of the fat from the ham. Score the top with $\frac{1}{4}$-inch cuts, crisscrossing the cuts at 1-inch intervals to create a diamond pattern. Set the ham in a roasting pan, add the cider to the pan and bake for 1 hour.

In a bowl, combine the orange marmalade, mustard, and sugar. Blend well. Brush the ham with half of the mixture. Bake for 45 minutes longer. Brush with the remaining glaze mixture and bake for 30 minutes more. Remove the ham from the oven and let it rest for 10 minutes for the juices to settle.

Present the ham on a large platter, garnished with the kale leaves. Carve at the table.

YIELDS MANY SERVINGS WITH LEFTOVERS

(continued)

....

WINE SUGGESTIONS

A FRESH RED BURGUNDY OR A
WHITE, SLIGHTLY SWEET
RHINE SPÄTLESE FROM
GERMANY ARE BEST BETS FOR
THE SMOKY TASTE OF HAM.

....

Corn bread

Coarsely ground cornmeal has a rich, nutty flavor that enhances the buttery taste of this very special loaf of bread. No yeast, no rising time, a very simple recipe.

$2^3/_4$ *cups coarsely ground cornmeal*
$1^3/_4$ *cups flour*
$^1/_2$ *cup sugar*
$1^1/_4$ *tablespoons baking powder*
$1^1/_2$ *teaspoons salt*
$2^1/_8$ *cups buttermilk*
18 tablespoons ($2^1/_4$ sticks) melted butter
3 eggs, lightly beaten

Preheat the oven to 375°F. Butter two $4^1/_2$-by-$8^1/_2$-by-3-inch pans.

In a large bowl, combine all the dry ingredients.

In another bowl, combine the moist ingredients. Pour the dry mixture into the liquid mixture and stir with a wooden spoon for about 5 minutes, making sure all the ingredients are well blended. Let the mixture stand for 20 minutes.

Divide the batter between the 2 pans. Smooth the tops and bake for 35 to 40 minutes, or until a toothpick inserted in the center of the bread comes out clean.

YIELDS 2 LOAVES

Roast rack of lamb

The pink, tender meat coated with a savory crust and marinated in a pungent sauce is just great. Have your butcher French the rib bones for you. This will help turn the lamb into a beautiful dinner party presentation.

2 racks of lamb, trimmed

THE MARINADE

3 garlic cloves, mashed
1 tablespoon finely chopped fresh rosemary
2 tablespoons soy sauce
$^{1}/_{2}$ cup dry sherry
1 teaspoon freshly ground black pepper

THE COATING

3 garlic cloves, crushed
1 teaspoon salt
$^{1}/_{2}$ teaspoon freshly ground black pepper
3 tablespoons Dijon mustard
$^{1}/_{2}$ cup finely chopped fresh flat-leaf parsley
$^{1}/_{2}$ cup fine bread crumbs
$^{1}/_{3}$ cup olive oil

$^{1}/_{2}$ cup veal or chicken stock (page 86 or 84)
Fresh rosemary sprigs for garnish

(continued)

Preheat the oven to 475°F.

Place the racks of lamb in a shallow dish. In a bowl, combine all the marinade ingredients and pour the mixture over the lamb. Set aside at room temperature for 30 minutes.

Saving the marinade, remove the racks of lamb to a roasting pan. Roast for 15 minutes.

In another bowl, combine the coating ingredients to make a paste. Spread the crumb paste all over the meat. Return the lamb to the oven and roast for 15 to 20 minutes longer. For rare lamb, your meat thermometer should read 125°, medium would be 135°. Transfer the racks to a serving platter and let them rest for 10 minutes.

Meanwhile, pour the chicken stock and reserved marinade into the roasting pan and set it over high heat. Cook, scraping up all the brown bits to get a richer taste. Boil hard for 1 minute. Strain the sauce into a sauceboat. Garnish the lamb with rosemary sprigs and serve it with the sauce on the side.

WITH 3 RIBS PER PERSON, YIELDS 4 SERVINGS

WINE SUGGESTIONS

A BIG RED FROM THE PIEDMONT REGION OF ITALY, SUCH AS A BAROLA OR A RED BORDEAUX, WILL GO WELL WITH THIS DISH.

Ragout of beef
with black olives

A zesty, richly satisfying casserole that's so comforting on a cold winter's eve. It's an easy, foolproof recipe that you'll find yourself making over and over again.

2 tablespoons olive oil

1 cup finely chopped pancetta

4 pounds boneless beef chuck, cut into 2-by-2-inch chunks

4 cups finely chopped onions

1 tablespoon minced garlic

3 tablespoons flour

1½ cups finely chopped carrots

1 fennel bulb, finely chopped

3 cups finely chopped plum tomatoes

1 teaspoon dried thyme

2 bay leaves

½ cup minced fresh flat-leaf parsley

1 tablespoon salt

1 teaspoon freshly ground black pepper

4½ cups red wine

3 cups sliced mushrooms

1 cup pitted black olives, packed in brine, drained

Preheat the oven to 350°F.

Heat the olive oil in a large heavy sauté pan. Add the pancetta and brown. Add the meat and, over high heat, allow it to brown for about 10 minutes, without stirring. Stir once and brown for 10 minutes longer. Add the onions and garlic and stir once. Cook the mixture for 5 minutes. Add the flour and stir to blend well. Add the carrots, fennel, plum tomatoes, then the thyme, bay leaves, parsley, salt, and pepper. Stir to blend. Pour in the wine and bring to a boil.

Transfer the mixture to a large casserole or roasting pan. Cover tightly and bake for 2 hours. Fold in the mushrooms and olives. Bake for 30 minutes longer. Serve hot.

YIELDS 6 SERVINGS
WITH PLENTY OF LEFTOVERS

WINE SUGGESTIONS

A RIOJA FROM SPAIN
OR A CHIANTI FROM
ITALY ARE GOOD
MATCHES FOR THIS
STURDY DISH.

Side dishes
for fall and winter

Winter is the season for leeks, cabbages, cauliflower, a wide variety of root vegetables, mushrooms, and squash. I must confess to using frozen peas, lima beans, and corn in the winter. The crops are quick-frozen immediately after picking, sealing in all the nutrients and flavor.

Winter is also the time to discover new ways of preparing various grains, such as barley, wild rice, and risotto. It is simple to bake a potato, add butter or sour cream and chives, and sometimes that is exactly what will hit the spot. In compiling the following recipes, my hope is to offer suggestions that might help you reach beyond the familiar and turn the ordinary into something exceptional.

Petit Pois are like children—you have to understand them.

JAMES DE COQUET

Butternut squash puree with fresh ginger

When fall arrives, I think of all the comfort foods that come with the season. This is definitely one of them.

> *2 large butternut squash (about 6 pounds total)*
> *2 cups water*
> *¼ cup peeled and chopped fresh ginger*
> *4 tablespoons (½ stick) hot melted butter*
> *1 teaspoon salt*
> *½ teaspoon ground white pepper*

Peel and remove the soft center of the squash. Reserve the seeds. Cut the squash into large chunks. Place in a heavy saucepan, add the water, and bring to a boil. Lower the heat and cook, covered, for 30 minutes, or until soft. Drain and spoon the cooked squash back into the same saucepan.

Place the ginger and hot butter in a blender and puree for 5 seconds. Add to the squash. Sprinkle with the salt and pepper. Using a hand-held potato masher, mash the squash until smooth. Serve hot.

YIELDS 6 SERVINGS

THE PUREE CAN BE PREPARED
A DAY AHEAD. SPOON IT INTO
AN OVEN-TO-TABLE
CASSEROLE, COVER, AND
REFRIGERATE. WHEN READY
TO SERVE, COVER WITH FOIL
AND BAKE IN A 375°F. OVEN
FOR 40 MINUTES, OR UNTIL
HEATED THROUGH.

SAUTÉED BUTTERNUT SQUASH SEEDS

PLACE THE SEEDS IN A SMALL
BOWL, ADD 1 TABLESPOON
OLIVE OIL, 1 TABLESPOON
HONEY, A PINCH OF DRIED
THYME, AND SALT AND PEPPER
TO TASTE. LET STAND AT
ROOM TEMPERATURE FOR 1
HOUR OR MORE. WHEN READY
TO SERVE, SAUTÉ THE SEEDS
IN A LITTLE CLARIFIED
BUTTER UNTIL THEY'RE
GOLDEN BROWN AROUND THE
EDGES. SPRINKLE THEM OVER
THE SQUASH PUREE JUST
BEFORE SERVING. OR SERVE
THE SEEDS WITH DRINKS
BEFORE DINNER.

Gratin of potatoes

This is a Loaves and Fishes specialty. Many of our customers drop off their empty casserole dishes early in the day and pick them up later, filled, hot, and ready to eat. We also make a Parsnip Gratin, which has a subtler, sweeter taste. Either one is an excellent complement for any broiled or grilled meat.

2 pounds baking potatoes, peeled and sliced thin
1 large garlic clove, minced
1 teaspoon salt
$^1/_2$ teaspoon freshly ground black pepper
1 cup heavy cream
$1^1/_2$ cups milk

Preheat the oven to 400°F.

Layer the potato slices in a casserole dish. Sprinkle with garlic, salt, and pepper. In a saucepan, bring the cream and milk to a boil. Pour over the potatoes and bake for 50 minutes, or until the potatoes are fork-tender.

YIELDS 4 SERVINGS

PÁRSNIP GRATIN

FOLLOW THE RECIPE FOR POTATO GRATIN, SUBSTITUTING 2 POUNDS PARSNIPS, PEELED AND CUT UP, FOR THE POTATOES. REDUCE THE BAKING TIME TO 45 MINUTES.

Creamed potatoes
with olive oil

2¹/₂ *pounds golden potatoes, peeled and halved*
4 garlic cloves, peeled
2 teaspoons salt
¹/₂ *cup milk*
¹/₄ *cup heavy cream*
¹/₂ *cup olive oil*
¹/₂ *teaspoon freshly ground black pepper*

Place the potatoes, garlic, and 1 teaspoon of the salt in a pot, cover with water, and cook for 15 to 20 minutes, or until the potatoes are tender. Drain.

In a small saucepan, heat the milk and cream.

In a bowl, mash the potatoes and garlic by hand with a potato masher. Add the heated milk mixture and mash until combined. Add the olive oil, the remaining 1 teaspoon of salt, and the pepper and mash until the potatoes are smooth and glossy. Serve hot.

YIELDS 6 SERVINGS

Corn pudding

Requested by our corn pudding–loving guests and customers.

> $^1/_2$ *pickled jalapeño pepper*
> *3 small Anaheim chilies*
> *3 cups fresh or frozen corn kernels*
> *5 eggs*
> *1$^1/_2$ cups cottage cheese*
> *$^3/_4$ cup heavy cream*
> *5 tablespoons melted butter*
> *6 tablespoons flour*
> *1 teaspoon baking powder*
> *1 tablespoon sugar*
> *2 teaspoons salt*

Preheat the oven to 375°F. Butter a 2-quart casserole.

In the bowl of a food processor, puree the jalapeño and Anaheim chilies. Add the corn and pulse 5 times.

Scrape the mixture into a bowl, add the eggs, and beat well to blend. Add the cottage cheese, heavy cream, and butter. Stir well. Add the flour, baking powder, sugar, and salt. Mix until the dry and wet ingredients are well combined.

Spoon the mixture into the casserole and bake for 45 minutes, or until the pudding is set.

YIELDS 6 SERVINGS

Leeks au gratin

We like to pour a light and delicious béchamel sauce over the vegetables just before serving.

> 1 tablespoon butter
> 4 leeks, white parts only, washed thoroughly, cut into
> $^1/_2$-inch rings

BÉCHAMEL SAUCE

> 4 tablespoons ($^1/_2$ stick) butter
> 3 tablespoons flour
> 1$^1/_2$ cups milk
> $^1/_2$ cup heavy cream
> 1 teaspoon salt
> $^1/_2$ teaspoon freshly ground black pepper
> *Preheat the broiler. Butter a 1$^1/_2$-quart casserole.*

In a large sauté pan, melt the butter and add the leeks. Sauté over low heat for about 15 minutes, or until they're just cooked through. Transfer the leeks to the casserole dish.

For the béchamel sauce, melt the butter in a medium-size heavy saucepan. Add the flour and, stirring constantly, cook the mixture over low heat for 2 minutes. Do not let it brown. Add 1 cup of the milk and continue stirring until the mixture is bubbling. Add the remaining milk and the cream and bring to another boil. Turn down the heat and, while stirring, allow the sauce to simmer for 1 minute. Add the salt and pepper. Pour the sauce over the leeks and stir to blend. Broil for 5 to 6 minutes, or until the top of the gratin is brown.

YIELDS 4 SERVINGS

Haricots verts with walnuts and walnut oil

Carefully prepared green beans are a complement to almost any main-course meat dish. Here is an especially easy and delectable way to serve them.

1¼ *pounds small green beans, trimmed*
2 *tablespoons butter*
3 *tablespoons walnut oil*
⅓ *cup coarsely chopped walnuts*
½ *teaspoon salt*
½ *teaspoon freshly ground black pepper*
1 *tablespoon fresh lemon juice*
2 *tablespoons finely chopped fresh parsley*

Bring a saucepan filled with water to a rapid boil. Drop in the green beans and cook, uncovered, for about 3 minutes, or until the beans are still crisp yet tender. Drain and set aside.

In a skillet, melt the butter over medium heat. Add the walnut oil and walnuts. Sauté for 1 minute. Add the beans and sauté for about 2 minutes, or until the beans are coated and heated through. Add the salt, pepper, lemon juice, and parsley. Stir well and serve hot.

YIELDS 4 SERVINGS

IF YOU PREFER SESAME
SEEDS, SIMPLY SUBSTITUTE
OLIVE OIL FOR THE WALNUT
OIL, ADD 2 TEASPOONS
TOASTED SESAME OIL, AND
REPLACE THE WALNUTS
WITH 2 TABLESPOONS
SESAME SEEDS.

Garlic-roasted cauliflower

1 large cauliflower
1 cup water
2 teaspoons salt
1 large garlic clove
3 tablespoons olive oil
1 tablespoon finely chopped fresh parsley

Preheat the oven to 450°F.

Cut the cauliflower into small florets. Place the florets in a saucepan, add the water, and bring to a boil. Lower the heat, cover, and simmer for 2 minutes. Drain. Place the partially cooked cauliflower in a bowl.

In a small bowl, mash the salt and garlic into a paste. Mix the paste with the olive oil and pour the mixture over the cauliflower. Toss well to blend. Spread the florets in one layer on a baking sheet and roast for 15 minutes. The florets should still retain some resistance when pierced with a knife.

Serve hot, sprinkled with the chopped parsley.

YIELDS 4 SERVINGS

Popovers
Potato Frittata
Orange Marmalade

Roast Lobster with Saffron Sauce
and Lima Bean Puree

Smoked Fish Platter

Baked Ham with Mustard and Orange Glaze

Beetroot Salad with Fresh Rosemary

Gravlax with Mustard Sauce

Swedish Meatballs with Capers and Dill

Whipped Cream with a Cinnamon Dusting

Macadamia Nut Tart

Ginger-Pumpkin Cake

Mocha Cake with Mocha Buttercream

Almond Butter Cookies

Nut and Jelly Cookies

Bohnen, birnen, und schinken

This delicious specialty of beans, pears, and ham originated in northern Germany. It's a dish my mother used to serve in deep, wide soup plates with slabs of buttered rye bread or peeled and cooked potatoes. Sweet, delicately salty, and substantial.

> 2 tablespoons olive oil
> 3 cups coarsely chopped onions
> 1 pound smoked ham, cut into bite-size pieces
> 3 cups chicken stock (page 84)
> 4 ripe pears, quartered and cored
> 1¹/₂ pounds green beans, trimmed and cut into 1-inch pieces
> 1 teaspoon salt
> ³/₄ teaspoon freshly ground black pepper

In a large heavy saucepan, heat the olive oil and sauté the onions over low heat for 5 minutes, until they're glossy. Add the ham and sauté for 5 minutes longer. Add the chicken stock and pears and bring to a boil. Lower the heat, cover the pan, and simmer for 5 minutes. Add the beans and cook, covered, for 15 minutes longer, or until the beans are done to your taste. Stir in the salt and pepper and serve.

YIELDS 4 SERVINGS

Oven-braised red cabbage

$^1/_4$ *pound finely chopped pancetta or bacon*

2 tablespoons olive oil

3 pounds (1 medium head) red cabbage, cut into fine strips

2 cups finely chopped onions

1 cup red wine

$^1/_4$ *cup light brown sugar*

$^1/_2$ *cup balsamic vinegar*

1 tablespoon salt

1 teaspoon freshly ground black pepper

Preheat the oven to 375°F.

In a large, heavy saucepan, sauté the pancetta for 5 to 6 minutes until almost all the fat is rendered. Add the remaining ingredients. Cover the pan with a tight-fitting lid and bring the cabbage to a boil. Stir to blend. Replace the lid and braise the cabbage in the oven for 1 hour. The cabbage should be crisp yet tender.

YIELDS 6 SERVINGS

THE CABBAGE CAN BE MADE
UP TO 4 DAYS AHEAD OF TIME
AND STORED IN THE
REFRIGERATOR. REHEAT,
COVERED, IN A 375°F. OVEN
FOR 35 TO 40 MINUTES.

Sauté of savoy cabbage

This is an excellent accompaniment for duck dishes, game, and roast pork.

4 tablespoons ($^1/_2$ stick) butter
1 small head Savoy cabbage, quartered, cored, cut
     into thin strips.
1 teaspoon caraway seeds
1 teaspoon grated lemon rind
1 tablespoon fresh lemon juice
$1^1/_2$ teaspoons salt
1 teaspoon freshly ground black pepper

In a sauté pan, melt the butter over low heat. Add the cabbage strips, then the rest of the ingredients, and cover the pan with a tight-fitting lid. Cook over medium heat for 8 minutes. The cabbage should not brown. Stir, then cover and cook for 2 minutes longer. The cabbage should be barely cooked and crunchy. Taste for seasoning and serve.

YIELDS 4 TO 6 SERVINGS

Roasted brussels sprouts and carrots

THE BRUSSELS SPROUTS

1¹/₂ pounds Brussels sprouts, trimmed
¹/₄ cup olive oil
1¹/₂ teaspoons kosher salt

THE CARROTS

1 pound carrots, peeled, cut into ¹/₂-by-2-inch sticks
1 tablespoon soy sauce
2 tablespoons olive oil
1 teaspoon kosher salt

THE GARNISH

Zest of 1 lemon
2 tablespoons finely chopped fresh parsley

Preheat the oven to 400°F.

Place the Brussels sprouts in a bowl and toss with the olive oil and salt. Transfer to a roasting pan, filling one side of the pan, saving the other side for the carrots.

In another bowl, toss together the carrots, soy sauce, olive oil, and salt. Tuck the carrots into the other side of the roasting pan.

Roast the vegetables for about 40 minutes. The Brussels sprouts should be dark, tender, and crisp. The carrots should be cooked through. To make a pretty presentation keep the vegetables separated when you spoon them into a serving dish. Sprinkle with the lemon zest and parsley.

Most winter vegetables
can be roasted in this
same manner: parsnips,
peeled and cut, or left
whole; any of the
squashes, such as acorn or
butternut; sweet potatoes,
fennel bulbs, even endive,
left whole, are delicious
roasted. The roasting time
will depend on how large
you cut the pieces and the
density of the vegetable.
However, as a general
rule, 30 to 40 minutes
should do the trick. To
test for doneness, pierce
the vegetables with a fork
after 30 minutes. You will
be the best judge of how
well-cooked they are.

Chanterelles, shallots, and peas

4 tablespoons (¹/₂ stick) butter
2 pounds shallots, peeled
¹/₃ pound chanterelle mushrooms, tough ends and
    stems removed
3 cups frozen petit pois
1 teaspoon salt
1 tablespoon finely minced fresh parsley
1 tablespoon fresh lemon juice

In a large sauté pan, melt the butter. Add the shallots and sauté over medium heat for 10 minutes, until they're brown.

Add the chanterelles. Turn the heat to high and sauté for 5 minutes longer. Add the peas. Stirring, sauté for 5 minutes more. Add the salt, parsley, and lemon juice. Stir again and serve hot.

YIELDS 6 SERVINGS

Pearl barley
with cremini mushrooms

Because of its unique nutty texture, pearl barley is an excellent side dish with lamb.

>   *4 tablespoons (¹/₂ stick) butter*
>   *1 cup pearl barley*
>   *5 cups chicken stock (page 84)*
>   *2 tablespoons olive oil*
>   *1 pound cremini mushrooms, sliced*
>   *³/₄ cup finely chopped shallots*

In a large, heavy saucepan, melt the butter. Add the barley and sauté, stirring, over a low heat for 5 minutes. Add the chicken stock and bring the mixture to a boil. Lower the heat, cover, and simmer for 1 hour and 15 minutes.

In a cast-iron skillet, heat the olive oil. Add the mushrooms and shallots. Sauté over medium-high heat for about 8 minutes. Fold the mushroom mixture into the cooked barley. Serve hot.

YIELDS 6 SERVINGS

Wild rice with toasted pecans and cranberries

All native-grown American products that, when combined, make a most delightful side dish to serve with roasted and grilled meats and poultry. This recipe is very easy and can be doubled successfully.

> *1 cup wild rice (6 ounces)*
> *4 cups water*
> *2 tablespoons olive oil*
> *1 cup finely chopped onions*
> *¼ cup dried cranberries*
> *Grated rind of 1 orange*
> *3 tablespoons fresh orange juice*
> *3 tablespoons coarsely chopped toasted pecans*
> *1 teaspoon salt*
> *½ teaspoon freshly ground black pepper*
> *2 tablespoons finely chopped fresh parsley*

In a saucepan, combine the rice and water and bring to a boil. Lower the heat, cover, and simmer for 35 to 40 minutes, or until the rice is crisp and tender. Drain and return the rice to the same saucepan.

In a skillet, heat the olive oil and sauté the onions over medium heat for about 8 minutes, until the onions are soft. Add to the rice. Add the remaining ingredients, and reheat briefly, stirring the rice. Spoon onto a dish and serve hot.

YIELDS 4 SERVINGS

Basmati rice pilaf

A small but long-grained Indian rice that has a light, fluffy yet nutty texture when baked in the oven. This is an excellent accompaniment to veal, meat, and chicken dishes that have a sauce, such as Blanquette of Veal or Chicken Breasts with Cider Sauce.

> 1 cup long-grain basmati rice
> 2 tablespoons olive oil
> $^1/_3$ cup finely chopped shallots
> 1 teaspoon salt
> 2$^1/_2$ cups chicken stock (page 84)

Preheat the oven to 350°F.

Wash and drain the rice to remove the outer starches. Set aside.

In an ovenproof saucepan, heat the olive oil and sauté the shallots over medium heat for 5 minutes, or until they're soft. Add the rice and stir to coat all the grains. Add the salt and the chicken stock. Bring to a boil, remove from the heat, cover with a tight-fitting lid, and place in the oven for 25 minutes. Cook until all the liquid is absorbed and the rice is tender.

YIELDS 4 SERVINGS

Risotto with white truffle oil

I like to use porcini or Portobello mushrooms with this particular recipe because of their smoky, woodsy taste.

3 tablespoons butter
2¹/₂ cups sliced wild mushrooms
1 tablespoon olive oil
¹/₃ cup finely chopped shallots
1¹/₄ cups arborio rice
³/₄ cup dry white wine
5 cups hot chicken stock (page 84)
1 teaspoon salt
¹/₄ cup white truffle oil
1 tablespoon chopped fresh chives

In a large skillet, melt the butter. When very hot, add the sliced mushrooms and sauté over high heat for 5 minutes. Remove from the heat and set aside.

In a large saucepan, heat the olive oil and sauté the shallots over medium heat until they turn glossy, about 5 minutes. Make sure not to brown them. Add the rice and the white wine. Turn the heat to high and stir until the wine has evaporated. Stirring constantly, add the chicken stock, 1 cup at a time. As each cup of stock is absorbed, add another, stirring and simmering for 18 to 20 minutes. Remove from the heat and stir in the sautéed mushrooms.

Spoon the risotto onto 4 heated plates. Drizzle 1 tablespoon of truffle oil over each serving and garnish with the chopped chives.

YIELDS 4 SERVINGS

Cheese, fruits, and salads
for after dinner

. . . .

Salads, especially with good cheese, are very important to a good meal. In general, fall and winter greens are much heartier, as are their dressings.

We serve escarole, endive, lolla rosa, chickory, trebiola, radicchio, spinach, romaine, and frisée. One of them, or any combination of 3 or 4, with a substantial dressing, produces a very special salad. Here are my favorite dressings:

Hazelnut oil salad dressing

1 egg yolk
1 tablespoon strong mustard
$1/2$ teaspoon salt
$1/4$ teaspoon freshly ground black pepper
1 tablespoon Calvados (apple liqueur)
2 tablespoons red wine vinegar
$1/3$ cup hazelnut oil

Combine all the ingredients in a container with a tight-fitting lid. Shake well. Pour over your salad, toss, and serve.

YIELDS A LITTLE OVER A CUP

Sherry vinegar and shallot dressing

2 large shallots, sliced
1 garlic clove
1 teaspoon salt
1 tablespoon mustard
$1/4$ cup sherry vinegar
$3/4$ cup olive oil

In a bowl, mash together the shallots, garlic clove, and salt. Mix with the mustard, vinegar, and olive oil. Pour over your salad and toss.

YIELDS 1 CUP

Soy vinaigrette

¹/₃ cup wine vinegar
¹/₃ cup peanut oil
¹/₄ cup soy sauce
2 tablespoons toasted sesame oil
Juice of 1 lemon
¹/₂ teaspoon freshly ground black pepper

In a bowl, combine the rice vinegar, peanut oil, soy sauce, toasted sesame oil, lemon juice, and freshly ground black pepper. Pour over a hearty salad and toss.

YIELDS 1¹/₂ CUPS

Balsamic vinaigrette

¹/₃ cup balsamic vinegar
²/₃ cup olive oil
¹/₂ tsp salt
¹/₂ tsp pepper

Combine all the ingredients in a container with a tight-fitting lid. Shake well. Pour over your salad, toss, and serve.

YIELDS 1 CUP

Cheeses

....

Cheeses also vary considerably during the fall and winter months. In early fall you can get aged goat cheese, made from the milk of animals who have grazed all summer on lush grass, clover, herbs, berries, and flowers. Many cheeses need to age at least three months, some as much as six months, in order to be at their best. That is why, even though there are excellent cheeses available in the winter, it is a treat when you find one that was produced from animals who fed from the earth rather than a bucket.

Keeping all this in mind, I've gathered together a list of cheeses that sell briskly at Loaves and Fishes and that we like to serve at the Inn with salads or fresh seasonal fruits, such as pears, apples, or grapes. To heighten the pleasure, we make sure there's a fresh loaf of crusty sourdough or French bread to offer around. Plain bread never seems to dignify the ripeness and beauty of cheese.

Reblochon *is a deeply flavorful, semi-soft cheese made from cow's milk;* Vacherin, *a highly prized monastery cheese, also made from cow's milk, is almost puddinglike in texture;* Brillat-Savarin, *a triple cream made from cow's milk is a dessert on its own;* Brin d'Amour, *made from sheep's milk, is semi-soft and savory, with an herb-crusted exterior;* Bucheron-Bougon, *a rich, tangy goat cheese with a crumbly texture is from the Poitou region;* Roquefort, *creamy with a spicy and powerful flavor, is made from sheep's milk and is one of the world's oldest cheeses;* Couloummiers, *a sheep's milk cheese from Normandy, is creamy and Brie-like;* Pecorino Romano, *a sheep's milk cheese from Italy, is sharp and tangy;* Pecorino Pepato, *from Tuscany, is a semi-firm cheese with black peppercorns;* Raclette, *a very hearty cheese, almost beeflike in flavor, is semi-firm and sliceable;* Fontina Val d'Aosta, *is semi-firm, tangy, and deliciously full flavored.*

I urge you to visit a good cheese store, look over the display, ask about the different cheeses, sample some, and buy one or two at a time. I promise you a new and delightful experience each time you do. Refrigerate the cheese until two hours before serving time. To enjoy its fullest flavor, cheese should be served at room temperature.

He who does not eat cheese will go mad.

<small>FRENCH PROVERB</small>

Desserts for fall and winter

*A*pples, plums, cranberries, all the fall fruits, together or apart, tucked into pies, layered over flaky tart shells, or poached in wine, topped with whipped cream, ice cream, or crème fraîche, are ideal seasonal desserts. But let us not forget the cakes, the trifles, the Rich Chocolate Bars, even a refreshing Pineapple Mousse thrown in as a surprise.

Winter is the time when one can go completely mad with desserts. Since the kitchen becomes, even more than ever, the center of activity, it seems right to have the savory aromas of roasting meats mingling with the sweet fragrances of dessert. And, even though we always plan a menu by deciding on a main course first, my love of desserts somehow edges its way through, and I often find myself anticipating the perfect climax to a marvelous dinner. If it is a rich meal with a creamy sauce, I know that by the end of it, my guests will truly appreciate something light *yet just rich enough to complement the main course. If the main course is less com-plicated, I tend to pull out all the stops on the dessert.*

The following recipes have been selected with loving care from my personal notebooks. Some were inspired by recipes passed on to me by my mother, who loved a great dessert as much as I do.

Baked fall fruit

We like to serve this mouth-watering compote in deep bowls with scoops of caramel or rum raisin ice cream.

> *4 tablespoons ($^1/_2$ stick) butter*
> *2 large tart apples, cut into eighths, cores removed*
> *3 ripe pears, cut into sixths, cores removed*
> *6 large ripe plums, cut in half, stones removed*
> *Grated rind of 1 orange*
> *$^3/_4$ cup sugar*

Preheat the oven to 400°F. Rub the butter over the bottom and up the sides of a baking dish large enough to hold all the fruit.

In a large bowl, combine the remaining ingredients and mix well.

Turn the mixture into the baking dish and bake, uncovered, until all the fruit is soft and baked through. Depending on the ripeness of the fruit, the baking could take anywhere from 30 minutes to 1 hour. When the fruit is done, remove the dish from the oven and set it aside to come to room temperature before serving.

YIELDS 4 SERVINGS

Caramel apple pie

As a family, we always go apple picking in the fall. When I return, I heap the apples into baskets and scatter them throughout the Inn, where their seductive aromas permeate the rooms and create a wonderfully homey atmosphere.

THE CRUST

1^3/$_4$ cups flour
6 tablespoons (^{3}/$_4$ stick) butter, cut into 6 slices
4 tablespoons (^{1}/$_2$ stick) margarine, cut into 4 slices
1 tablespoon granulated sugar
1 tablespoon fresh lemon juice
6 tablespoons cold water

THE FILLING

8 medium apples, Cortland or Macintosh, peeled, cored, and sliced
2^1/$_2$ tablespoons flour
Juice of ^{1}/$_2$ lemon
^{1}/$_2$ teaspoon ground cinnamon
^{1}/$_2$ cup light brown sugar, packed
^{1}/$_2$ cup raisins

THE TOPPING

1 cup light brown sugar, packed
^{1}/$_4$ cup flour
^{1}/$_4$ teaspoon ground cinnamon
4 tablespoons (^{1}/$_2$ stick) softened butter

To make the crust, place the flour, butter, margarine, and sugar in the bowl of a food processor fitted with the metal blade. Pulse for 5 seconds. With the motor running, add the lemon juice and water. Process until the pastry starts to cling together. Remove the pastry from the bowl and shape it into a ball. Cover with plastic wrap and chill for 30 minutes.

Preheat the oven to 400°F. Butter a 9½-inch pie plate.

Turn the dough onto a floured surface and roll it out into a 13-inch circle. Fit the round into the pie plate.

For the filling, in a large bowl, combine all the ingredients and blend well. Transfer the filling to the unbaked pastry shell.

In the same bowl, mix the topping ingredients until crumbs form. Sprinkle the crumbs over the pie filling. Trim the crust to ½ inch beyond the pie plate and flute the edges. Bake for 1 hour, or until the crust is browned and the apples are tender and bubbling.

YIELDS 6 GENEROUS SERVINGS

Apple tart

Use Cortland, Macintosh, or any tart fresh apple for this easy-to-prepare dessert. A chilled Vanilla Chantilly Cream (see box) poured over the warmed tart is something I heartily recommend.

THE CRUST

1^1/$_4$ cups flour
1 teaspoon sugar
^{1}/$_2$ teaspoon baking powder
6 tablespoons (^{3}/$_4$ stick) cold butter, diced into cubes
1 egg yolk
2^1/$_2$ tablespoons cold water

THE FILLING

3^1/$_2$ pounds apples, peeled, halved, and cored
3 tablespoons butter
^{1}/$_4$ cup sugar

THE GLAZE

^{1}/$_2$ cup apple jelly
1 tablespoon water

To make the crust, place the flour, sugar, and baking powder in the bowl of a food processor fitted with the metal blade. Add the cubes of butter. Pulse 5 times. Add the egg yolk and, with the motor running, add the water. Process just until the dough is crumbly. Remove from bowl and, by hand, knead the pastry into a ball. Cover in plastic wrap and chill for 30 minutes.

Preheat the oven to 375°F.

Roll the pastry into a 12-inch round. Fit it into a 9-inch round tart pan. Prick the bottom liberally with a fork. Bake for 8 minutes. Cool for 10 minutes.

For the filling, place the apples, cut side down, on a cutting board. Retaining their shape, cut each apple downward into very thin slices. Keeping the sliced apple intact, carefully transfer it to the pastry shell. Slant the apple slightly so the cuts are just visible. Continue in the same manner with the remaining apple halves until the pastry shell is covered and piled high with apples. Dot with the butter, sprinkle with the sugar, and bake for 45 to 50 minutes, or until the apples are just cooked and are a nice brown color. Cool for 15 minutes.

In a saucepan, heat the apple jelly with the water. Brush the glaze over the apple tart. Serve warm or at room temperature.

YIELDS 6 TO 8 SERVINGS

VANILLA CHANTILLY CREAM
BEAT TOGETHER 1 CUP HEAVY
CREAM, A FEW VANILLA BEAN
SEEDS, AND 1 TEASPOON
SUGAR TO THE CONSISTENCY
OF SLIGHTLY WHISKED EGG
WHITES. SERVE CHILLED.

Cranberry crumb tart

At times we substitute raspberries or cherries, and the result is the same—a piquant tart that puts an exclamation point on the end of a meal. Try it warm, with a dollop of sweetened whipped cream or your favorite ice cream.

THE TART

2 cups flour
1¹/₂ tablespoons sugar
¹/₂ teaspoon salt
¹/₂ teaspoon baking powder
6 tablespoons (³/₄ stick) cold butter, cut into very small pieces
2 small egg yolks
¹/₄ cup water

THE FILLING

4¹/₂ cups fresh or frozen cranberries
³/₄ cup sugar
Grated rind of ¹/₂ orange

THE TOPPING

³/₄ cup flour
³/₄ cup sugar
¹/₂ teaspoon ground cinnamon
6 tablespoons (³/₄ stick) cold butter, cut into small pieces

To make the crust, place the flour, sugar, salt, baking powder, and butter in the bowl of a food processor and pulse 5 times. Add the egg yolks and water. Process until the dough forms a ball. Remove the dough, cover with plastic wrap, and chill in the refrigerator for 30 minutes.

Preheat the oven to 400°F. Butter a 9-inch tart pan with a removable bottom.

Transfer the chilled dough to a lightly floured surface and roll the dough out to ¼-inch thickness. Fit it into the tart pan, pressing the dough against the bottom of the pan and up the sides.

For the filling, in a bowl, combine the cranberries, sugar, and orange rind. Transfer to the uncooked crust, making sure the sugar is evenly distributed among the berries.

For the topping, place all the ingredients in a bowl and rub the mixture with your fingertips until it starts to cling together. Sprinkle the crumb mixture evenly over the cranberry filling.

Bake for 45 minutes, or until the fruit is bubbling and the crumbs turn golden brown. Cool for 2 hours before serving.

YIELDS 6 TO 8 SERVINGS

Macadamia nut tart

The tartness of the cranberries seems a perfect partner to the richness of the macadamia nuts. We serve this scrumptious tart with Vanilla Chantilly Cream (page 331) or Crème Anglaise (page 158).

THE CRUST

1¹/₂ cups flour
2 tablespoons granulated sugar
¹/₈ teaspoon salt
10 tablespoons (1¹/₄ sticks) cold butter, cut into small pieces
1 egg yolk
¹/₂ cup cold water

THE FILLING

1¹/₂ cups macadamia nuts
1¹/₂ cups fresh or frozen coarsely chopped cranberries
8 tablespoons (1 stick) melted butter
3 eggs
1 cup light brown sugar
²/₃ cup light corn syrup
1 teaspoon vanilla extract

For the crust, place the flour, sugar, and salt in the bowl of a food processor. Add the butter and pulse 4 times. Add the egg yolk and, with the motor running, add the cold water in a stream through the feed tube. Process until the dough is crumbly. Turn the dough onto a work surface and gather the crumbs into a ball. Cover with plastic wrap and refrigerate for 30 minutes.

Preheat the oven to 375°F.

Roll the dough out to ¹/₄-inch thickness. Fit it into two 4-by-12-inch tart pans, or one 10-inch round tart pan, with removable bottoms. Freeze the unbaked tart shells for 15 minutes, then bake for 10 minutes. This process will keep the tart dough from shrinking. Remove the shells from the oven and lower the oven temperature to 350°.

For the filling, scatter the nuts and cranberries into the partly baked shell.

In a bowl, beat together the butter, eggs, brown sugar, corn syrup, and vanilla. Pour the mixture evenly over the nuts and cranberries.

Bake for 35 to 40 minutes, or until the filling has set.

Serve warm or at room temperature.

YIELDS 6 TO 8 SERVINGS

IF MACADAMIA NUTS ARE
NOT AVAILABLE, USE
HAZELNUTS OR PECANS.
RASPBERRIES CAN ALSO BE
SUBSTITUTED FOR THE
CRANBERRIES.

Rich chocolate bars
with warm chocolate sauce

This is definitely a recipe for all those confirmed chocolate fanatics. We like to arrange the bars around a scoop of ice cream, then ladle warm chocolate sauce over the top. We have also served these chocolate gems as a centerpiece with other cookies. They are always the first to go.

6 ounces unsweetened chocolate

12 tablespoons (1$^1/_2$ sticks) butter

6 eggs

3 cups sugar

1 tablespoon vanilla extract

2 teaspoons instant espresso powder

$^1/_2$ teaspoon salt

1$^1/_2$ cups flour

WARM CHOCOLATE SAUCE

8 ounces semi-sweet chocolate

10 tablespoons (1$^1/_4$ sticks) unsalted butter

2 teaspoons vanilla extract

2 teaspoons Kahlúa (coffee liqueur)

Preheat the oven to 350°F. Butter a 9-by-13-by-1$^1/_2$-inch cake pan.

Combine the chocolate and butter in a bowl and place it in the oven for about 15 minutes, until they've melted. Remove and cool to room temperature.

Using an electric mixer, in a bowl, beat the eggs, sugar, and vanilla extract until creamy. Add the melted chocolate mixture and the instant espresso. Beat to blend well. Add the salt and flour. Beat until no traces of flour are visible.

Pour the batter into the cake pan and bake for 30 minutes, or until just set. Don't overbake. Cool in the pan, then transfer to the refrigerator until very cold. This should take about 6 hours. Overnight would be best.

To make the chocolate sauce, preheat the oven to 350°F. Combine all the sauce ingredients in a bowl and place in the oven for about 15 minutes to melt. Stir the mixture gently until very smooth. Do not whisk or beat. This will yield about 1¼ cups.

Cut the chocolate into bars of a size that suits your taste. We usually cut them into 1-by-2-inch or 2-by-2-inch pieces and serve them teepee style around a scoop of ice cream with the warm chocolate sauce drizzled over the top.

YIELDS ANYWHERE FROM 24 TO 48 BARS
OF CHOCOLATE DELIGHT

Hazelnut trifle

A truly festive dessert enjoyed by all ages. It looks best presented in a footed, glass or crystal trifle dish, decorated with a sprig of holly. We use our own SandKage for this recipe because it has just the right amount of sweetness and a perfect texture for soaking up the sherry. It's best to make the pastry cream a day or two in advance and store it, covered, in the refrigerator until you're ready to assemble all the ingredients. Once you have everything ready, it goes very fast.

THE PASTRY CREAM

9 egg yolks
1 cup sugar
6 tablespoons cornstarch
3 cups milk
Seeds of $\frac{1}{2}$ vanilla bean

1 pound cake or SandKage (page 346)
1 cup dry sherry
$1\frac{1}{2}$ cups strawberry preserves
1 cup heavy cream
1 tablespoon sugar
$\frac{1}{2}$ cup coarsely ground hazelnuts plus 8 whole
   hazelnuts for garnishing

To make the pastry cream, in a bowl, beat the egg yolks, sugar, and cornstarch with a wire whisk until they're light and creamy. Add the milk and stir. Pour the mixture into a heavy saucepan and bring to a boil over medium heat, stirring constantly, for about 10 minutes, until the pastry cream is very thick and bubbling. Transfer the mixture to a bowl and stir in the vanilla seeds. Cover with plastic wrap and chill overnight.

To assemble the trifle, cut the cake into $^3/_4$-inch-thick slices. Arrange the slices inside a trifle dish. Spoon half the sherry over the slices, making sure they will soak evenly. Spread the slices with some of the preserves. Cover with 2 cups of pastry cream.

In a bowl, beat the heavy cream with the sugar until it's firm. Spread half the cream over the pastry cream. Sprinkle with half the ground hazelnuts. Repeat the process of layering: cake, sherry, preserves, and pastry cream.

Spoon the remaining whipped cream into a pastry bag fitted with a tip. Pipe it on the top of the trifle in a decorative pattern. Sprinkle with the remaining ground hazelnuts and top with the whole hazelnuts.

YIELDS 6 TO 8 SERVINGS

Mocha cake
with mocha buttercream

A gorgeous centerpiece for your holiday buffet table. Chocolate and coffee! Delicious tastes that seem to be universally enjoyed. The cake can be made up to 3 days ahead and stored, wrapped, in the refrigerator. To serve, uncover the cake and bring it to room temperature.

THE CAKE

¹/₂ cup unsweetened cocoa powder

2 teaspoons ground cinnamon

1 teaspoon instant espresso powder

³/₄ cup strong brewed coffee, at room temperature

12 tablespoons (1¹/₂ sticks) softened butter

2 cups sugar

1 teaspoon vanilla extract

³/₄ cup sour cream

1³/₄ cups flour

³/₄ teaspoon baking soda

4 egg whites

THE MOCHA BUTTERCREAM

1 cup sugar

¹/₄ cup water

5 egg whites

¹/₂ teaspoon cream of tartar

24 tablespoons (3 sticks) softened butter

3 tablespoons unsweetened cocoa powder

2 tablespoons instant espresso powder

3 tablespoons Kahlúa (coffee liqueur)

16 chocolate coffee beans

Preheat the oven to 325°F. Lightly butter a 9-inch springform pan.

For the cake, in a small bowl, combine the cocoa, cinnamon, espresso, and brewed coffee.

In another bowl, cream the butter, sugar, and vanilla extract with an electric mixer until light and fluffy. Add the cocoa/coffee mixture and the sour cream. Beat at low speed until smooth. Add the flour and baking soda. Beat until well combined.

In a clean bowl, beat the egg whites until they form soft peaks. Using a rubber spatula, fold the egg whites into the mocha batter. Pour the batter into the springform pan. Bake for 50 to 55 minutes, or until a toothpick inserted into the center comes out clean. Cool the cake in the pan.

To make the buttercream, place ³/₄ cup of the sugar and the water in a saucepan and bring to a boil. Stir once and boil the mixture for 5 minutes longer. Remove from the heat and set aside.

Using an electric mixer, beat the egg whites with the remaining ¹/₄ cup of sugar and the cream of tartar until they hold soft peaks. With the motor running, slowly pour in the sugar syrup. Continue beating until the syrup cools down somewhat. Add small amounts of butter at a time, continually beating, until all the butter has been incorporated.

In a separate bowl, mix together the cocoa powder, espresso powder, and Kahlúa. Pour the mixture into the whipped buttercream. Beat until just combined.

Transfer the cake to a large flat plate, and cut the cake horizontally into 3 layers. Spread the mocha buttercream over the bottom layer. Place the second layer on top of that and spread it with more buttercream. Add the top layer and cover it with buttercream, spreading it evenly over the surface and down the sides of the cake.

Fit a decorative tip into a pastry bag and fill the bag with the remaining buttercream. Pipe a design of your choice on the top of the cake. Garnish with the chocolate coffee beans and serve.

The cake can be made a whole day ahead of time, covered with a dome top, so as not to disturb the icing, and chilled in the refrigerator.

YIELDS 10 TO 12 SERVINGS

Pineapple mousse

A refreshing surprise at the end of a meal. It's great with Warm Chocolate Sauce (page 336) drizzled over the top.

1 small ripe pineapple
$^1/_2$ cup plus 2 tablespoons sugar
3 tablespoons fresh lemon juice
3 egg whites
2 cups heavy cream

Peel the pineapple and cut it into quarters. Remove and discard the hard center core. Cut one quarter into $^1/_4$-inch cubes and set aside. Cut the remaining pineapple into chunks and place in the bowl of a food processor. Add $^1/_2$ cup of the sugar and the lemon juice and puree until smooth. Transfer to a shallow bowl and freeze the puree for 1 hour.

In a bowl, beat the egg whites until they're frothy. Add the 2 tablespoons of sugar and beat until glossy. Remove from the mixing bowl and set aside. Add the cream to the same bowl and whip until soft peaks hold. Fold the egg whites and cream into the partly frozen pineapple puree along with the pineapple cubes.

Spoon the mousse into 6 individual glasses and freeze until ready to serve.

YIELDS 6 SERVINGS

Plum kuchen

❧

Although Italian plums have a very short season, between late summer and early fall, they're still worth waiting for. These particular plums, with their deep purple color and sweet, firm flesh, lend moisture and a deliciously tangy taste to this cake. It's a plum kuchen for many occasions. We serve it for afternoon tea or coffee, or for breakfast. Try it with lightly whipped cream or vanilla ice cream. Delicious.

8 tablespoons (1 stick) softened butter
1/2 cup plus 3 tablespoons sugar
1 teaspoon vanilla extract
4 eggs
1 1/4 cups flour
1 teaspoon baking powder
1 pound fresh Italian plums, cut in half and pitted

Preheat the oven to 350°F. Butter a 9-inch springform pan.

In a bowl, cream the butter and 1/2 cup of the sugar with an electric mixer until light in color. Add the vanilla. Add 1 egg at a time, beating well after each addition. Add the flour and baking powder and mix at low speed until smooth.

Scrape the batter into the springform pan. Arrange the plums on top of the batter in a circular pattern, cut side up. Sprinkle with the remaining 3 tablespoons of sugar. Bake for 45 to 50 minutes, or until a toothpick inserted in the center comes out clean. Serve warm or at room temperature.

❧

YIELDS 6 TO 8 SERVINGS

Ginger-pumpkin cake

A creation that everyone seems to enjoy, children and adults alike. It looks so pretty when served up as part of a holiday dessert buffet. Tall, sugary, sending out the most welcoming spicy bouquet. If there are any leftovers, they can be wrapped and stored in the refrigerator for up to a week.

> 4 eggs
> 1 cup safflower oil
> 2$^1/_2$ cups granulated sugar
> 2 cups pumpkin puree
> 3$^1/_2$ cups flour
> $^1/_2$ teaspoon baking soda
> 2 teaspoons baking powder
> $^1/_2$ teaspoon salt
> 2 teaspoons ground ginger
> 1 teaspoon ground cinnamon
> $^1/_4$ teaspoon ground cloves
> $^1/_2$ teaspoon freshly grated nutmeg
> 1 cup raisins
> $^2/_3$ cup coarsely chopped walnuts
> $^1/_4$ cup confectioners' sugar for dusting

Preheat the oven to 350°F. Butter a 9-by-4$^1/_2$-inch Turks head or bundt pan with a 12-cup capacity.

In a bowl, beat the eggs, safflower oil, and sugar with an electric mixer for about 3 minutes, until creamy. Add the pumpkin puree and mix to blend. Add 3 cups of the flour, the baking soda, baking powder, salt, ginger, cinnamon, cloves, and nutmeg. Mix at low speed until the batter is smooth and well blended.

Separately, combine the remaining $\frac{1}{2}$ cup of flour with the raisins and walnuts. Fold this into the batter. Spoon the batter into the cake pan.

Set the pan into the middle of the oven and bake for 1 hour and 10 to 15 minutes, or until a toothpick inserted into the cake comes out clean. Remove the cake from the oven and let it set for 30 minutes.

Using a knife, loosen the top edge of the cake. Invert the cake into a plate and let it cool completely for 6 hours or overnight. When ready to serve, dust the cake with confectioners' sugar.

YIELDS 10 TO 12 SERVINGS

SandKage

I was introduced to this fine-textured cake by my husband's aunt after he and I were first engaged. She lived in a walk-up apartment in the heart of Kiel and served us this lovely cake with delightful cups of strong coffee. After she had finished, she sat back and lit up a cigar, then a common practice among women who considered themselves fashionable. I had never seen a woman smoke, let alone a cigar. To this day I can't think of SandKage without smiling and thinking of her puffing away in her large comfortable chair.

> *16 tablespoons (2 sticks) softened butter*
> *1¼ cups granulated sugar*
> *4 eggs*
> *1 tablespoon rum*
> *Grated rind of 1 lemon*
> *1¾ cups flour*
> *⅓ cup potato flour or cornstarch*
> *2 teaspoons baking powder*

THE GLAZE

> *1 cup confectioners' sugar*
> *3 tablespoons fresh lemon juice*
> *1 tablespoon rum*

Preheat the oven to 350°F.

Using an electric mixer, in a bowl, cream the butter and sugar together until light. Add the eggs, one at a time, beating well after each addition. Add the rum, lemon rind, potato flour, and baking powder. Beat at low speed until the ingredients are well combined.

Spoon the batter into a 9-by-5-by-3-inch loaf pan. Bake in the center of the oven for 1 hour, or until a toothpick inserted in the center of the cake comes out clean. Cool for 15 minutes. Invert the cake onto a plate, then turn it right side up and cool completely.

For the glaze, in a bowl, combine the confectioners' sugar, lemon juice, and rum. Beat until smooth. Pour the glaze over the cake.

YIELDS 8 TO 10 SERVINGS

YOU CAN PREPARE THIS
CAKE UP TO 1 WEEK IN
ADVANCE. AFTER THE
GLAZE IS SET AND THE
CAKE IS COMPLETELY
COOLED, COVER IT IN
PLASTIC WRAP AND STORE
IN THE REFRIGERATOR.

A fine orange cake

We serve this sweet, moist cake with whipped cream. In the summer, we top it with fresh fruits and sweetened cream.

> *2 large or 3 small oranges*
> *12 tablespoons (1½ sticks) softened butter*
> *1¾ cups granulated sugar*
> *3 eggs*
> *1¼ cups flour*
> *½ cup cornstarch*
> *1½ teaspoons baking powder*

THE GLAZE

> *1 cup confectioners' sugar*
> *¼ cup fresh orange juice*

Preheat the oven to 325°F. Butter a 9-inch springform pan.

Peel the oranges. Cut the peel into 2-inch pieces. Remove and discard the white pith. Cut the oranges into quarters. Place the peel and flesh in the bowl of a food processor and process until smooth. There should be approximately 1½ cups of puree. Set aside.

Using an electric mixer, beat together the butter and sugar for 5 minutes, until the mixture is pale and creamy. Add the eggs, one at a time, beating well after each addition. Add the orange puree and mix just to combine. Add the flour, cornstarch, and baking powder. Mix at low speed until smooth.

Spoon the batter into the springform pan and bake for 1 hour 10 minutes, or until a toothpick inserted in the center comes out clean.

For the glaze, in a bowl, beat the confectioners' sugar and orange juice until all lumps have disappeared. Pour the glaze over the warm cake and cool to room temperature before removing it from the pan.

YIELDS 8 TO 10 SERVINGS

Almond butter cookies

2 cups unbleached white flour

1 cup sugar

$^{1}/_{2}$ teaspoon baking powder

12 tablespoons (1$^{1}/_{2}$ sticks) cold butter, cut into 12 pieces

2 eggs

1 teaspoon almond extract

1 teaspoon vanilla extract

$^{3}/_{4}$ cup slivered almonds, with their skins

Preheat the oven to 350°F.

In the bowl of a food processor, combine the flour, $^{2}/_{3}$ cup of the sugar, the baking powder, and butter. Process for 10 seconds, until the butter is mixed in. Add 1 egg, both extracts, and pulse 3 times. Turn the dough onto a work surface and, using your hands, form it into a ball.

Shape the dough into 3 long rolls, each $^{3}/_{4}$ inch thick. Arrange them on an ungreased baking sheet. Press down lightly on each roll to slightly flatten the top.

Beat the remaining egg with a fork and brush it over the dough. Sprinkle with the remaining $^{1}/_{3}$ cup of sugar. Press the almonds on top of each roll.

Bake for 15 to 20 minutes, or until the flattened rolls are slightly browned. While still warm, cut each flattened roll diagonally into 1-inch-wide cookies. Leave the cookies on the baking sheet until cool.

YIELDS 3 DOZEN COOKIES

Peanut cookies

At Loaves and Fishes we have huge glass jars filled with a variety of very large cookies. Since we opened our doors, we have had to refill the peanut cookie jar over and over each day. This recipe is for our loyal customers and our guests at the Inn, who enjoy a good cookie.

> *8 tablespoons (1 stick) softened butter*
> *$1/2$ cup granulated sugar*
> *$1/2$ cup light brown sugar*
> *$1/2$ teaspoon vanilla extract*
> *1 egg*
> *1 cup flour*
> *1 teaspoon baking powder*
> *1 cup shelled salted peanuts*
> *2 ounces semi-sweet chocolate, melted and cooled (optional)*

Preheat the oven to 350°F. Butter a baking sheet.

In a bowl, cream the butter and sugars with an electric mixer until the mixture is light. Add the vanilla extract and egg. Beat well. Add the flour, baking powder, and peanuts. Blend well.

Drop rounded tablespoons of batter, 2 inches apart, onto the baking sheet. Bake for about 10 minutes, or until the cookies are light brown. Cool. Drizzle the melted chocolate over the cooled cookies. Store in a cool, dry place.

YIELDS ABOUT 30 COOKIES

Nut and jelly cookies

A must on our holiday cookie plate!

> 12 tablespoons (1¹/₂ sticks) butter
> ¹/₃ cup sugar
> ¹/₂ teaspoon vanilla extract
> 2 eggs, separated
> 1¹/₂ cups flour
> 1 cup finely chopped hazelnuts
> 7¹/₂ teaspoons red currant jelly

Preheat the oven to 375°F. Butter a baking sheet with a tablespoon of the butter.

Using an electric mixer, in a bowl, cream together the remaining butter and the sugar until they're light in color. Add the vanilla and egg yolks and mix well. Add the flour. Mix at low speed until well combined.

In a separate bowl, lightly beat the egg whites with a fork until a few bubbles appear on the surface. Spread the chopped hazelnuts on a plate. Shape the dough into 1-inch balls. Dip each ball into the egg whites, coating all sides, then roll them carefully in the chopped hazelnuts, coating them lightly.

Place the pastry balls 1 inch apart on the baking sheet. With your thumb, press a ¹/₄-inch indentation in the top of each ball. Bake for 12 to 15 minutes, or until the cookies are light brown. Remove from the oven and, while the cookies are still hot, fill each indentation with ¹/₂ teaspoon of red currant jelly. When cool, store in an airtight container or cookie jar.

YIELDS ABOUT 30 COOKIES

Index